CHILDHOOD SEXUAL ASSAULT VICTIMS: LONG-TERM OUTCOMES AFTER TESTIFYING IN CRIMINAL COURT

Jodi A. Quas
Gail S. Goodman
Simona Ghetti
Kristen W. Alexander
Robin Edelstein
Allison D. Redlich
Ingrid M. Cordon
and
David P. H. Jones

WITH COMMENTARY BY
Jeffrey J. Haugaard

Willis F. Overton
Series Editor

MONOGRAPHS OF THE SOCIETY FOR RESEARCH IN CHILD DEVELOPMENT

Serial No. 280, Vol. 70, No. 2, 2005

 **Blackwell**
Publishing   *Boston, Massachusetts   Oxford, United Kingdom*

CHILDHOOD SEXUAL ASSAULT VICTIMS: LONG-TERM OUTCOMES AFTER TESTIFYING IN CRIMINAL COURT

CONTENTS

COMMENTARY

ABSTRACT

We report a longitudinal study of long-term outcomes of participating in criminal cases following child sexual abuse (CSA). In the 1980s, 218 child victim/witnesses took part in a study of short-term sequelae of legal involvement. Approximately 12 years later, 174 of them, as well as a comparison group of 41 matched individuals with no CSA history, were interviewed about their mental health and legal attitudes. Being young when the legal case started was associated with poorer later adjustment. Additionally, even when controlling for psychological problems at the start of the legal case and other familial, CSA, and life stressors, testifying repeatedly in childhood predicted poorer current functioning. These associations were often moderated by the severity of both the CSA and the perpetrator's sentence: Testifying repeatedly in cases involving severe abuse, and not testifying when the perpetrator received a light sentence, predicted poorer current mental health. In partial contrast to the mental health results, being older when the case began and the perpetrator receiving a lenient sentence predicted more negative feelings about the legal system. In addition, not having testified when the perpetrator received a light sentence predicted more negative legal attitudes. Individuals' emotional reactions while waiting to testify and while actually testifying were also associated with their current mental health and attitudes toward the legal system: Greater distress predicted poorer adjustment, especially in individuals who were adolescents when they went to court. Greater distress also predicted more negative attitudes. Finally, when the former CSA victim/witnesses were compared with individuals with no CSA history, the former reported poorer adjustment and more negative feelings about the legal system. Results have implications for multilevel-transactional models of development, for understanding developmental sequelae of legal involvement following childhood trauma, and for social policy concerning the treatment of child victim/witnesses.

I. INTRODUCTION

This *Monograph* describes a prospective longitudinal study of child sexual abuse (CSA) victims who were involved in criminal prosecutions. The study is an extension of previous research on the behavioral adjustment and legal attitudes of 4–17-year-old victim/witnesses. That research was described in a prior *Monograph of the Society for Research in Child Development* (Goodman et al., 1992). The earlier study afforded a unique opportunity to examine an important yet rarely studied stressor experienced by scores of child victims—testifying in criminal court.

The Goodman et al. (1992) study addressed the questions of whether testifying while facing the accused in court was traumatizing to children in the short term, and whether children's reactions to testifying differed as a function of their developmental stage. In the present *Monograph*, we examine whether, and under what conditions, mental health and attitudinal sequelae associated with legal participation are maintained over a period exceeding 10 years. How do children's age and developmental level at the time of legal involvement relate to their later mental health and attitudes about the legal system, both in general and with respect to their particular legal case? Years after a legal trial, was testifying in criminal court traumatizing or empowering? Does not having had the opportunity to testify in court seem, in retrospect, to have been beneficial or harmful?

Surprisingly, little is known from scientific research about how legal involvement, over and above maltreatment per se, affects children's long-term mental health and legal attitudes. It is well documented that maltreatment itself challenges and often damages developing socioemotional and cognitive systems that play important roles in the emergence and timing of normal developmental processes. Children who have experienced maltreatment master important developmental milestones, such as maintaining a secure attachment to a parent (Cicchetti & Lynch, 1993; Egeland, Yates, Appleyard, & Van Dulem, 2002) and establishing healthy relationships with peers (Hoffman-Plotkin & Twentyman, 1984), less well than their counterparts who were not maltreated. Moreover, risk factors (e.g., family

1

dysfunction) associated with child maltreatment at various ecological levels (Bronfenbrenner & Morris, 1998) interfere with normal development and with successful resolution of stage-appropriate developmental tasks (Cicchetti & Toth, 1995; Sameroff, Seifer, Zax, & Barocas, 1987). Consequently, children who have been maltreated have a greater likelihood of negative developmental outcomes, including psychopathology (Cicchetti & Toth, 1995), even before they face stressors inherent in the criminal justice system. However, it remains unknown whether legal involvement adds to children's long-term risk of poor outcomes or aids their healing process following abuse.

An examination of developmental pathways of maltreated children who become involved in the legal system can improve scientific understanding of normal and abnormal psychological development. Such an investigation is also important, however, from a legal perspective. For example, the Goodman et al. (1992) study was cited pivotally by the U.S. Supreme Court (Maryland v. Craig, 1990) and affected the interpretation of the 6th Amendment of the U.S. Constitution as applied to children. The 6th Amendment dictates the right of the accused to face-to-face confrontation with witnesses, including child victims of sexual abuse. This right assures the accused of the opportunity to cross examine a child victim/witness with the defendant in view, often in relatively close proximity to the child or, in principle, with the accused actually conducting the cross examination, regardless of the severity of the assault, the relationship to the defendant (e.g., the accused may be the child's father), or victim's level of fear. In Maryland v. Craig (1990), however, the Court ruled that, under certain circumstances (e.g., if children are too scared to communicate), children could testify via closed-circuit television rather than facing the accused in open court. Thus, the Goodman et al. (1992) findings had a powerful effect. Studies of the long-term outcomes, rather than just short-term outcomes, for child victim/witnesses who testify in court hold important potential to influence future Constitutional interpretation and legal norms.

For the current follow-up study, we used a prospective-longitudinal design to examine the long-term outcomes for the CSA victims who had been involved in criminal prosecutions approximately 12–14 years earlier. We specifically examined trauma-related psychopathology, general mental health, and legal attitudes—overall and in relation to children's age at time of legal involvement. Strengths of our study include not only its prospective, longitudinal design, but also several other important features. First, we extended the former research design by including three groups of participants: The two groups of children originally involved in the Goodman et al. (1992) study—CSA victim/witnesses who testified in criminal court and CSA victim/witnesses who were involved in prosecutions but did not testify—and a matched control group of nonabused children, for whom we had childhood measures of behavioral adjustment. Comparisons between testifiers and nontestifiers allowed us to examine long-term outcomes specific to children who testified. Comparisons between CSA victims formerly involved in criminal prosecutions and individuals with no history of CSA permitted us to examine long-term outcomes related to CSA and legal involvement more generally. These comparisons were conducted while statistically controlling for childhood behavioral adjustment. Second, the range of ages in childhood during which study participants had been exposed to CSA and subsequent legal involvement was substantial, enabling us to investigate developmental differences in former victims' long-term outcomes. Third, advances in the study of child maltreatment have led to the development of measures of trauma-related psychopathology specific to CSA. We therefore included such measures in the current study—for example, measures of post-traumatic stress disorder (PTSD), dissociation, and defensive avoidance of trauma memories.

Before describing our study, we first discuss legal issues concerning the prosecutorial involvement of child victim/witnesses. We then highlight theoretical considerations relevant to the study by situating it within a multilevel-transactional model of development (Bronfenbrenner's ecological theory), studies of risk factors in development, particularly ones relevant to developmental psychopathology (Cicchetti & Rogosch, 1999; Overton & Horowitz, 1991), and studies of the psychology of procedural justice (Tyler, 1994). We then review prior psychological research concerning how developmental and legal factors relate to mental health and legal attitudes, and we consider potentially confounding factors (e.g., family risk factors) that could qualify our findings.

LEGAL CONSIDERATIONS

Beginning in the late 1970s, there was an upsurge of reporting of sexual crimes against children. The increase was, in part, a result of mandated CSA reporting laws being implemented nationwide and of research indicating that CSA was much more pervasive than formerly believed (Finkelhor, 1984; Russell, 1986). Furthermore, legal changes governing CSA cases (e.g., dropping corroboration requirements, eliminating the presumption that young children were incompetent to testify) allowed increasing numbers of child victim/witnesses into the criminal justice system. One dilemma faced by those who cared for, treated, or worked professionally with child victims—a dilemma that still exists today—was the need to protect children from potential "secondary victimization" by the legal system, which might exacerbate the trauma caused by sexual abuse itself (e.g., Glaser & Spencer, 1990; Katz & Mazur, 1979). Like adult victim/witnesses, child victim/witnesses may be subjected to long delays before trial; repeated continuance of trial dates; hostile and humiliating cross examination; and public in-court discussion of personal, traumatic, and embarrassing events. Such experiences are believed by laypersons and professionals to be traumatic for many children (e.g., Batterman-Faunce & Goodman, 1993).

Legal experts, including members of the U.S. Supreme Court (Coy v. Iowa, 1988), argue that short-term negative effects of testifying are common for many victim/witnesses. Such effects, it is claimed, are unavoidable given the nature of the U.S. legal system, which guarantees the 6th Amendment right to confrontation (see Melton, Goodman, Kalichman, Levine, Saywitz, & Koocher, 1995). But what if these adverse outcomes persist? Evidence relevant to long-term psychological effects of criminal court participation is clearly needed. Accommodations for child witnesses might be more likely to be introduced in legal cases if research demonstrates that testifying, or extensive legal involvement, is associated with long-term negative outcomes. Alternatively, it is possible that legal involvement, although stressful in the short term, might be beneficial in the long term. The procedural justice literature indicates that both adults and children have more positive attitudes toward decisions when they are more rather than less involved in making those decisions (e.g., Gold, Darley, Hilton, & Zanna, 1984; Hicks & Lawrence, 1993; Sigelman & Waitzman, 1991; Tompkins & Olejnik, 1978; Tyler & Lind, 2001). Most of the developmental research on procedural and distributive justice, however, has focused on hypothetical scenarios (e.g., stories) or laboratory-based distribution of resources (e.g., pretend money) rather than on children involved in real legal cases. To the extent that the procedural justice findings generalize to legal experiences, it is possible that children grow to understand the importance of the role they played in the legal process and feel proud to have had their day in court, despite having originally experienced the act of testifying as stressful. If so, by adulthood, testifying should be perceived as more beneficial than not testifying.

Unfortunately, there is little prospective research on the outcomes for adults who, as children, were involved in the legal system as victims of crime. From a practical perspective, the lack of research is unfortunate because assumptions about the psychological effects of legal involvement influence both legal decisions (e.g., whether or not to prosecute a case or use protective measures in court) and parental decisions (e.g., about reporting suspected abuse to authorities). From a theoretical perspective, research concerning the reactions of children of various ages to legal involvement adds to our understanding of developmental and other risk factors associated with long-term psychological and attitudinal reactions to stressors.

Finally, it is important to differentiate effects of abuse from effects of legal involvement. There is already an important research literature on the associations between CSA, as well as other stressful childhood experiences

4

(e.g., divorce, child physical abuse, parental death, and child illness), and developmental outcomes. This literature reveals that childhood trauma, including sexual assault, places many children at risk for subsequent adverse reactions. Most studies have not, however, factored out possible effects of legal involvement when examining childhood trauma. Nor have studies examined potential reactions to legal encounters that go beyond the effects of abuse. When such effects are confounded, it is difficult to identify the detrimental sequelae of abuse per se and to determine whether and when the legal system provides useful intervention and when it inflicts additional trauma.

THEORETICAL CONSIDERATIONS

The hypotheses tested in the present study were derived not only from the extant (albeit few) studies concerning outcomes following legal involvement, but also from multilevel-transactional developmental theory and empirical studies of risk factors that influence human development. Because of the importance of the latter two topics for understanding our study design and analytic approach, each is reviewed in turn.

Multilevel-Transactional Theories and Risk Factors in Development

As Masten and Wright (1998) note, "Theories of child maltreatment, as well as empirical data, point to the importance of models that encompass multiple systems in dynamic interaction as they influence and are influenced by individual development. Such multifactorial models represent, for maltreatment research as well as the field of child development more generally, first steps toward a more comprehensive understanding of individual functioning in the context of the many systems directly or indirectly connected to the child, including family, peers, community, culture, and society" (p. 8). A similar statement could be made concerning theory and research on legal involvement following maltreatment. In particular, consistent with Bronfenbrenner's (1979) seminal conceptualization of multiply interacting systems that affect development, the legal context provides a special opportunity to study development as it is affected by a unique and notoriously stress-inducing social institution (e.g., the criminal justice system) as well as by multiple potentially interacting systems (e.g., the child, family, and legal systems).

Sameroff and Chandler's (1975) transactional model similarly asserts that developmental outcomes at any point in time are a result of the continuous, dynamic interplay among child behavior, caregiver responses to the child's behavior, and environmental variables that influence both the

5

child and the caregiver. For those who dare to enter it—or who have no choice but to do so—the legal system is a potentially important context that influences both the child and the caretaker. Sameroff and Chandler further argue that transactions between the child and the caretaking environment can break or maintain links between earlier trauma (in this case, maltreatment) and later behavioral problems, and that such transactions must be taken into account if successful predictions about development and developmental outcomes are to be made. Transactions between the child and the legal system may similarly break or maintain the links between earlier CSA trauma and later psychopathology (see also Cicchetti & Lynch, 1993).

Within multilevel models, personal and environmental factors that adversely affect development are called "risk factors," which are contrasted with factors that promote adaptive outcomes in the face of adversity ("protective" factors), and factors that foster well-being regardless of adversity ("promotive" factors). A number of conceptual frameworks and empirical studies in the field of developmental psychopathology have emphasized the central role that risk factors play in contributing to negative developmental outcomes in children (e.g., Masten & Coatsworth, 1998; NICHD Early Child Care Research Network, 2004; Rutter, 1979; Sameroff, Seifer, Baldwin, & Baldwin, 1993; Werner & Smith, 1992). Research on children's legal involvement provides an opportunity to examine the role of particular risk factors in development.

Risk factors are often conceptualized in terms of individual (i.e., child level), proximal (e.g., family level), and distal (e.g., neighborhood- or community level) influences (Bronfenbrenner, 1979). Within the context of the present research on CSA-related legal involvement, individual factors of particular relevance to long-term mental health and attitudinal outcomes include children's age, gender, and pre-prosecution mental health. Proximal risk factors include a host of family-related influences, some of which co-occur with CSA (e.g., neglect or emotional maltreatment by parents, not being close to one's mother, maternal mental illness, witnessing domestic violence, and parental abandonment), as well as various life stressors and traumas more generally. Given our concern with CSA victims, it is important to consider specific CSA-related risk factors separately from other proximal risk factors. Distal factors of primary interest in the present study include children's legal experiences, such as testifying, the case being dismissed, or a guilty verdict being rendered.

Within the transactional-theory tradition, "cumulative risk" refers to the number of specified risk factors, typically each dichotomously scored, to which a person has been exposed. Examples of the types of risk factors considered in cumulative risk indices include severe marital discord, low socioeconomic status, paternal criminal activity, maternal emotional disorders, stressful life events, cold maternal–child interactions, and admission into the care of local authorities (e.g., foster care; Rutter, 1979; Rutter & Quinton, 1977; Sameroff et al., 1993). It has been proposed that the accumulation of risk factors, rather than any one risk factor, determines child outcomes (Rutter, 1979; Sameroff et al., 1987). This hypothesis has been verified in numerous studies: The more risk factors, the worse the outcomes in terms of child mental health (Rutter, 1979; Williams, Anderson, McGee, & Silva, 1990; Sameroff et al., 1987), social competence (Furstenberg, Cook, Eccles, Elder, & Sameroff, 1999), and cognitive performance (Sameroff, Siefer, Barocas, Zax, & Greenspan, 1987).

Despite the potential importance of cumulative risk, debate continues about how best to conceptualize this construct and decide which factors to include (e.g., Burchinal, Roberts, Hooper, & Zeisel, 2000; Deater-Deckard, Dodge, Bates, & Pettit, 1998; NICHD Early Child Care Research Network, 2004). Risk factors tend to co-occur, and some may be more influential than others in the case of particular adverse outcomes. Moreover, several recent studies suggest that domains of risk factors (e.g., child risk factors, family/parenting risk factors) convey important information that is lost in cumulative risk indices (e.g., Deater-Deckard et al., 1998; but see NICHD Early Child Care Research Network, 2004). In the present study, we were primarily interested in how a specific legal risk, testifying, directly and in conjunction with CSA victim/witness age or developmental stage at entry into the criminal justice system, relates to long-term outcomes. Nevertheless, we also considered several additional risk domains to account for other possible influences on our sample.

PREDICTORS OF LONG-TERM OUTCOMES

In this section we review predictors of long-term outcomes for CSA victims who experienced legal involvement. We first discuss research on sequelae of CSA and how CSA victims' risk for adverse outcomes varies with development. Second, we describe how specific characteristics of a legal case may relate to individuals' long-term mental health problems and negative attitudes toward the legal system. Third, we review other potentially important factors at the individual- and proximal-system levels that need to be considered when examining psychological outcomes for individuals involved as children in criminal court cases because of CSA.

CSA, Development, and Risk

In investigations of the sequelae of childhood trauma, it is imperative to take into account the developmental period within which the trauma occurred. Insofar as legal involvement is distressing, requires at least some

7

comprehension of legal processes, and is demanding of coping resources, children's developmental level should affect long-term outcomes following CSA-related legal involvement. In our study, the CSA precipitated the legal case and already placed children at risk for adverse outcomes. Thus, we first review what is known about effects of CSA and then consider age-related changes in such effects. Such knowledge is necessary to understand how legal involvement exacerbates or ameliorates age-related sequelae. We then discuss age at the time of the legal case, first as it relates to long-term mental health outcomes and second as it relates to current legal attitudes.

Sequelae of CSA

CSA is associated with a host of mental health and social problems, including feelings of low self-worth and low self-efficacy; depression and other forms of negative affect; and heightened aggressiveness and sexual acting out (see Berliner & Elliot, 2002; Kendall-Tackett, Williams, & Finkelhor, 1993; Trickett & Putnam, 1993, for reviews). Adverse outcomes of trauma that are especially relevant to CSA include post-traumatic stress, defensive avoidance of trauma memories, and heightened dissociation (Briere, Elliot, Harris, & Cotman, 1995; Browne & Finkelhor, 1986; Kendall-Tackett et al., 1993). Additionally, although maltreated and non-maltreated children do not generally differ in focus of moral judgment on Piagetian tasks (e.g., focusing on the outcome of events rather than on intention; Fontaine, Salvino-Pardieu, Crouzet, & Pulford, 2002; Smetana, Toth, Cicchetti, Bruce, Kane, & Daddis, 1999), in several other research paradigms, maltreatment (potentially including CSA) has been found to place children at risk for hostile attributional biases, social problem-solving deficits, and anticipation of rejection that overgeneralizes to new contexts (Dodge, Bates, & Pettit, 1990; Downey & Feldman, 1996).

Insofar as CSA itself affects long-term functioning, it is necessary to control for such influences when examining how characteristics of a CSA legal case relate to later mental health and legal attitudes. Elements of CSA that have important implications for long-term consequences of legal involvement include severity of the assault and whether it was intrafamilial or extrafamilial (see Berliner & Elliot, 2002; Kendall-Tackett et al., 1993). Severe abuse (e.g., abuse that occurs over a long time period or involves more invasive sexual acts) is likely to leave a child particularly vulnerable should he or she experience other traumas, including those associated with legal involvement generally and testifying in court specifically. Severe abuse is also potentially more traumatic and embarrassing for a child to recount, possibly repeatedly, to authorities. Intrafamilial abuse (e.g., incest) may place a child at greater risk of adverse outcomes following legal involvement because, for example, of the conflict associated with having to testify against a loved one. Such CSA features may interact with certain legal experiences (i.e., testifying) to result in particular harm to children. Also, such CSA features are often correlated with other important factors (e.g., older children are more likely to suffer severe CSA; girls are more likely than boys to be involved in intrafamilial CSA cases; Goodman et al., 1992; Gray, 1993). It is therefore important to take multiple factors into consideration.

Age and CSA

It is widely believed that traumas occurring in early childhood can have adverse effects that persist throughout life (e.g., Egeland et al., 2002). Animal studies of early trauma, from which causality can be inferred, confirm that early trauma can alter developmental trajectories and hence have a distinctly different impact than trauma experienced later in life (e.g., Sanchez, Ladd, & Plotsky, 2001). Research on humans suggests that, although younger children may express fewer adverse responses than do older children in the short term, younger children's long-term outcomes may indicate greater early emotional harm (Rutter, 1983).

Evidence for these claims specifically concerning CSA, however, has been mixed. Regarding mental health, for example, some studies indicate more adverse psychological effects of CSA when it occurs at earlier ages (e.g., Finkelhor, 1979; Russell, 1986), but other studies either suggest that older children are more adversely affected or find no age differences (e.g., Quas, Goodman, & Jones, 2003; Tufts New England Medical Center, 1984). Regarding attitudes, Dodge et al.'s (1990) research suggests that maltreatment that occurs at an early age will have the most detrimental and lasting effect on children's attitudes and social information processing because relevant core beliefs and behavioral tendencies are typically formed during the first 8 years of life (Dodge & Price, 1994; Ehrensaft, Cohen, Brown, Smailes, Chen, & Johnson, 2003).

In general, the inconsistent findings concerning age and outcomes following CSA may reflect differences in measures used and samples studied. Alternatively, the inconsistencies may indicate that the effects of CSA are negative regardless of age, although perhaps for different reasons. Moreover, use of chronological age instead of measures of developmental stages and transformations may complicate the detection of effects (Overton, 1998). Unfortunately, the delineation of developmental change related to CSA remains elusive. Finally, variability in findings may reflect the need to consider other risk factors in children's lives, including, as we discuss next, legal experiences.

Like CSA at a young age, legal involvement during an early developmental period may be especially detrimental to later mental health. Theory and research on socioemotional development indicate that young children have limited ability to cope effectively with stressors; they require considerable assistance from supportive adults (Bowlby, 1980; Ferguson, 1979; Quas et al., 2003; Rutter, 1983). This may cause younger children to be more easily intimidated and stressed in legal settings (e.g., when they are required to testify without the presence of potentially supportive family members who have been excluded from the courtroom). The resulting distress, above and beyond that caused by the CSA itself, may increase the emotional harm done to child victim/witnesses. Further, cognitive developmental theories indicate that young children lack the intellectual capability to understand a system of complex social relations that need to be characterized at an abstract level (e.g., justice, legal system; Kohlberg, 1969; Piaget, 1932). Even at the level of concrete representations (e.g., attorney, judge), comprehension of complex relations among such representations are beyond most young children's mental abilities (Case, 1991; Fischer, 1980). Combined with young children's limited knowledge concerning legal professionals and procedures (Block, Oran, Goodman, & Oran, 2005; Davis, Quas, Horowitz, & Lyon, 2005; Flin, 1992; Saywitz, Jaenicke, & Camparo, 1990; Warren-Leubecker, Tate, Hinton, & Ozbek, 1989), their cognitive immaturity leads to the prediction that young children compared with older ones (e.g., adolescents) will experience greater confusion regarding their legal experiences. We already know that increased confusion about the legal system is associated with increased distress in the short term (Goodman, Tobey, Batterman-Faunce, Orcutt, Thomas, & Sachsenmaier, 1992); such distress may persist over time.

Children's developmental level at the time of legal involvement should be considered when evaluating their later perceptions of the former CSA legal case and their later attitudes toward the legal system generally. Although relatively few researchers have studied actual child victims' legal attitudes (but see Sas, 1993), researchers have examined legal attitudes in normative samples of adults (e.g., perceptions of the legal system's fairness; Ashworth & Feldman-Summers, 1978; Thibaut & Walker, 1975; Tyler, 1994; Tyler & Degoey, 1995; Umbreit, 1989) and fairness judgments in normative samples of children and adults (e.g., Enright, Enright, & Lapsley, 1981; Gold, Darley, Hilton, & Zanna, 1984; Hicks & Lawrence, 1993;

McGillicuddy-DiLisi, Watkins, & Vinchur, 1994; Piaget, 1932). Piaget (1932) proposed that young children's egocentrism leads them to view "right" and "fairness" in terms of obedience to the will of authority and that young children focus exclusively on outcomes rather than intentions in making moral judgments. However, empirical findings generally suggest that even young children can make fairly complex distinctions, including the ones between intentions and outcomes, provided the information is presented in a clear and memorable fashion (Peterson, 1995).

Direct application of such developmental findings to child victims involved in legal cases is difficult, however. Because of older children's more advanced cognitive development and knowledge compared with that of younger children, older children better understand the functioning of the legal system (Block et al., 2005; Davis et al., 2005). Older children also have greater appreciation of the significance not only of the CSA itself, but of their own legal situation as well (even though their appreciation of their legal situation is still incomplete). Thus, older children are more likely to realize the serious implications involved for themselves, their family, other potential victims, and the defendant (Cashmore & Bussey, 1989; Melton & Berliner, 1992; Saywitz, 1989; Warren-Leubecker et al., 1989). Finally, older children are treated more harshly when they testify in court (i.e., they experience harsher cross examination) and are more likely to have their credibility questioned (Bottoms & Goodman, 1994; Whitcomb et al., 1991), which may increase their negative feelings about having testified. Findings from the Goodman et al. (1992) study confirmed this possibility. The adolescents, not the younger child victim/witnesses, expressed the most negative attitudes about their legal experience.

Summary

Children's developmental level when participating in a CSA criminal case has several implications for their long-term mental health and attitudinal responses. First, consistent with prior research on exposure to trauma, being young when a legal case takes place, which is itself compounded by being young when the abuse occurred, should be associated with the highest levels of mental health problems, problems that could persist into adulthood. Second, based on cognitive developmental theory and research, as well as the few studies that have examined legal attitudes among actual child victims, being older at the time of the legal case is likely to be associated with more negative attitudes about the system.

Legal System and Risk

One of the main goals of the present research was to examine how child victim/witnesses' well-being and legal attitudes vary depending not only on age, but also on specific legal experiences, especially testifying. Only a handful of studies, most of which concern short-term reactions, have examined mental health and attitudinal outcomes for children involved in CSA prosecutions. Five studies have investigated sequelae following longer delays (e.g., a few years), although none has focused on outcomes across the transition to adulthood. Overall, studies suggest that legal involvement is associated with emotional distress and negative attitudes, at least for a subset of children (e.g., DeFrancis, 1969; Goodman et al., 1992; Oates & Tong, 1987; Runyan, Everson, Edelsohn, Hunter, & Coulter, 1988; Whitcomb et al., 1991). We next discuss the specific characteristics of children's legal experiences that appear to be important in determining adverse outcomes. Again, our discussion focuses first on mental health outcomes and then on attitudinal outcomes.

Legal Characteristics and Mental Health

The most studied of the components of child victim/witnesses' legal experiences that might affect mental health is testifying. Public discussion of intimate sexual details, harsh cross examination, preparing oneself emotionally to take the stand only to have the court proceeding continued to a new date, and facing the defendant in court are features that adults, as well as children, often find distressing (e.g., Freshwater & Aldridge, 1994; Grey, 1993; Sahjpaul & Renner, 1988). CSA prosecutions, in particular, often rely heavily on children's testimony because of lack of corroborative evidence (Goodman, Quas, Bulkley, & Shapiro, 1999), putting additional pressure on children to take the stand.

Research confirms that testifying, especially repeatedly, is associated with greater distress during and soon after a CSA prosecution. Whitcomb et al. (1991), for instance, found that testifying multiple times, being on the witness stand for a longer time, and being treated harshly in the courtroom (factors that were combined to form an index of the level of distress associated with children's courtroom experience) predicted ill effects in CSA victims, especially among those who were older at the time of the case. In the research (described in depth later) that served as the foundation for the present study, Goodman et al. (1992) compared the behavioral adjustment of child victim/witnesses who testified in their CSA legal case with that of child victim/witnesses who were involved in a CSA legal case but did not testify. The nontestifiers were matched to the testifiers on key demographic

12

(e.g., age) and abuse (e.g., type of sexual acts) characteristics. Although most children's adjustment improved over time, regardless of whether they testified, a subset of testifiers continued to evince high levels of behavioral problems months after testifying. The strongest predictor of continued problems was testifying multiple times. In contrast, Berliner and Conte (1995) reported that the anticipation of testifying, rather than testifying itself, was associated with increased distress. This finding suggests that, even if children do not testify, preparing to testify (e.g., waiting at the courthouse) may lead to adverse mental health problems later.

In the aforementioned studies, the associations between testifying and distress were examined in the short term. As mentioned, a few studies have also examined how testifying relates to well-being over time. Runyan (as cited in Whitcomb et al., 1991) followed a small group of adolescents involved in CSA cases and found that testifying more than once predicted, in adolescence, negative long-term outcomes, such as teenage pregnancy, dropping out of school, and suicide attempts. In a second study, Bill (1995) examined the personality, behavioral characteristics, and school performance of 12 children who testified because of CSA, 17 alleged CSA victims who did not testify, and 30 children who reportedly had not been abused. The delay between testifying and the interview was 4 years. The children who testified had the lowest scores on self-concept, self-control, and discipline. However, because the children were all from the same preschool, and there was one single alleged molester, the generalizability of the findings to other types of cases is questionable. Somewhat different results were obtained in a third long-term and particularly comprehensive study conducted by Sas (1993), who found that testifying was unrelated to current well-being in a group of 126 CSA victims/witnesses followed 3 years after verdicts were rendered in Canadian cases. It should be noted, however, that all of the children participated in a Child Witness Preparation Program and thus received considerable support from program staff. Children's experiences in this program may partially explain the lack of associations between testifying and later adjustment. Also, Sas did not investigate whether frequency of testifying was related to children's later distress, and research suggests that testifying repeatedly may be particularly detrimental. In a fourth long-term study, Oates and Tong (1987) interviewed 49 CSA victims in Australia 2.6 years after their cases were referred to a hospital for evaluation. Only six of the children had testified in court. Among the 21 cases that resulted in juvenile or criminal prosecution, 18 nonoffending parents indicated that their child was very upset immediately after the hearings, and 12 indicated that, even 2.6 years later, their child was still upset about the legal experience. Additionally, parents of children whose cases went to court were more likely than parents of children whose cases did not go to court to report that their child had behavioral problems at school.

It is also possible that, at least for some children, not testifying is even worse in the long run than is taking the stand. This outcome would be especially expected when the case is dismissed or the perpetrator receives a light sentence. In such situations, children may regret not having had their day in court, especially years later when they have more perspective generally and knowledge about the criminal justice system specifically.

Aside from testifying, a number of other legal risk factors have been implicated as damaging to child victims' mental health. These factors include number of interviews, lack of maternal support at the time of the CSA legal case, delays and continuances of court hearings and trials, and case outcome (Berliner & Conte, 1995; Goodman et al., 1992; Henry, 1997; Runyan et al., 1988; Sas, 1993). Lack of maternal support stands out as a particularly important risk factor. For instance, Sas (1993) reported that the most important predictor of better adjustment at follow-up was maternal support, whereas child age was not a significant predictor in her study. Also, some (nonoffending) parents may be hostile to the prosecution or see the entire process as harmful to their children. To the extent that mothers are often also harmed by the prosecution (in terms of emotional strain, reduced family income, children removed from home, reminders of their own trauma histories), they may not be able to provide the level of emotional support needed by their children.

Two other legal risk factors concern the amount of contact with legal professionals and the outcome of the case. Increased contact with legal professionals (e.g., detectives, prosecutors), which is likely to be correlated with more interviews, has been associated with increased distress (e.g., Berliner & Conte, 1995). However, Henry (1997) found that, among children involved in juvenile and/or criminal court, having a trusting relationship with a legal professional predicted a reduced number of trauma symptoms. Finally, Sas (1993) reported that case outcome was related to CSA victims' mental health, with better adjustment being associated with a guilty verdict. Of note, few studies have examined how different characteristics of a legal case interact with each other or with age to predict later functioning. In particular, to better understand the potential long-term consequences of legal involvement, it is necessary to examine how the act of testifying, directly and in conjunction with other legal risk factors and children's developmental level, relates to witnesses' mental health over time.

Legal Characteristics and Attitudes

Regarding legal attitudes, the most consistent findings from previous studies indicate that children have more negative attitudes toward the legal system if their case results in a dismissal or a not-guilty verdict, if they are subjected to multiple interviews, if they are older, and if they are female

14

(Goodman et al., 1992; Sas, 1991; Tedesco & Schnell, 1987). For example, Tedesco and Schnell (1987) obtained 48 (out of 120 mailed) questionnaires completed either by child victims or knowledgeable adults (e.g., parents or social workers) following legal involvement because of CSA. Victims' ages ranged from 4 to 22 years; 81% were female. Testifying in court, enduring numerous interviews, being female, and experiencing intrafamilial abuse were associated with more negative attitudes toward the legal system. Unfortunately, Tedesco and Schnell did not report the delay between court involvement and participation in the study, which appeared to be long for some and short for others. In Sas's (1991, 1993) study, despite the child victims having participated in the Child Witness Preparation Program, many still had negative perceptions of their court experiences and considerable fears about testifying. Moreover, in the short term (Sas, 1991), developmental differences were found in the child victims' fears of testifying, with older children voicing more fears than younger children, and older children expressing a different set of fears (e.g., older children were more afraid of being accused of lying and of people thinking they were "weird"; younger children were more afraid of being sent to jail themselves). In Sas's (1993) follow-up study, which took place 3 years after the children's court appearances, comparable age analyses were not performed. However, Sas documented a number of comments that highlight, anecdotally, some children's continued negative feelings: "All I remember is that it had to be the hardest thing in my life to do," "I remember sitting in the chair, feeling sick and upset and not being able to eat and having daydreams that he [the defendant] would jump up and kill me in court," "It was terrifying," and "I remember crying a lot" (pp. 108–113). The largely descriptive nature of Sas' follow-up study precludes inferences regarding whether such perceptions of testifying significantly varied as a function of the children's age or developmental level.

Summary

Although relatively few long-term studies have been conducted, an overall impression from the short- and long-term research emerges, suggesting that: (a) courtroom testimony, especially when a child repeatedly takes the stand, is associated with worse mental health and more negative feelings about the legal system; (b) anticipation of testifying, as distinct from actually testifying, is related to increased distress; (c) older children and females may be especially at risk for negative legal attitudes; and (d) less severe sentences are associated with greater levels of distress and more negative attitudes toward the legal system.

Despite this convergence of findings, drawing definitive conclusions from existing research about associations between legal experiences and mental health or attitudinal outcomes is difficult for several reasons, including nonrandom assignment to groups (e.g., children with more mental health problems might be more likely to testify), low participation rates, lack of statistical control over potentially correlated variables (e.g., gender and type of abuse, abuse severity, and courtroom testimony), use of nonstandardized measures, studying small samples of children of limited age ranges, and/or lack of precourt measures of adjustment. Moreover, none of the studies systematically examined delays as long as 14 years, possibly missing important changes in perceptions of legal experiences across the transition from childhood to adulthood. Nor did most studies include a comparison group of nonabused children and control for personal and familial variables unrelated to the abuse or legal experiences. By addressing some of these limitations, the present study adds considerably to previous research in revealing the conditions under which children's legal experiences relate to increased (or, potentially, decreased) mental health problems and negative legal attitudes over time.

Individual and Proximal System-Level Factors and Risk

Although our study is focused mainly on developmental and legal factors, we consider these in conjunction with other possible influences on long-term mental health and legal attitudes. Consistent with multilevel-transactional developmental theories, these influences can be organized around individual (e.g., gender) and proximal (e.g., family) risk factors.

Individual

In addition to developmental factors, other individual-level characteristics that have implications for long-term outcomes following CSA-related legal involvement include gender and pre-prosecution mental health.

First, regardless of legal involvement, females tend to express emotional problems in terms of internalizing symptoms, whereas males tend to express them in terms of externalizing symptoms (Jackson & Warren, 2000; Leadbeater, Kuperminc, Blatt, & Hertzog, 1999; Maughan & Rutter, 1998). This differential expression of internalizing and externalizing symptoms increases with development (younger boys and girls tend to exhibit similar rates of both types of problems; e.g., Kraemer, Measelle, Ablow, Essex, Boyce, & Kupfer, 2003; Leadbeater et al., 1999). CSA exposure is one factor that increases girls' and boys' differential expression of internalizing and externalizing symptoms (Friedrich & Reams, 1987; Livingston, 1987; Pyle & Goodman, 1988). To the extent that participation in a legal case is an additional stressor over and above the CSA itself, females may show an increase in internalizing symptoms and males an increase in externalizing symptoms as a function of the extent of legal involvement experienced. Regarding legal attitudes, as mentioned, results of former studies indicate that female children, especially adolescents, express more negative feelings about legal involvement than male children (e.g., Goodman et al., 1992). Insofar as this negativity continues throughout the transition to adulthood, females may continue to harbor negative attitudes.

Second, an important predictor of adult mental health is childhood mental health (e.g., Messer, Maughan, Quinton, & Taylor, 2004; Rudd, Joiner, & Rumzek, 2004), indicating that it is important to take children's mental health into account before they become involved in a legal case when attempting to draw inferences about long-term outcomes following their CSA-related legal experiences. Without taking into account pre-prosecution mental health, inferences about any later differences are severely limited. In addition, children who at the start of a prosecution are more disturbed, perhaps as a result of CSA, might also be more vulnerable to the stress of legal involvement (e.g., Feiring, Taska, & Lewis, 1999; Friedrich, Urquiza, & Beilke, 1986). Presumably, a child whose mental health is already fragile would have more difficulty dealing with such stressors as numerous interviews, continuances of trial dates, and testifying repeatedly.

Family

A central feature of both Bronfenbrenner's (1981) and Sameroff and Chandler's (1975) multilevel-transactional models of developmental outcomes is the primary emphasis on the role of caregivers' and families' responses to children. A large body of research confirms the importance of the family environment, particularly parents' responsivity, for children's well-being (e.g., Gilliom, Shaw, Beck, Schonberg, & Lukon, 2002; Koop, 1989; Rohner, 2004; Steidl, Horowitz, Overton, & Rosenstein, 1992). For example, parenting is related to children's ability to regulate their emotions and behavior (Gilliom et al., 2002; Maugh & Cicchetti, 2002; Parke, 1995; Reimer, Overton, Steidl, Rosenstein, & Horowitz, 1996). Furthermore, negative parent–child relationships are associated with children's poor mental health in the wake of a variety of stressful events (Elder & Caspi, 1988; Elder & Conger, 2000; Rutter, 1971), including CSA (e.g., Conte & Berliner, 1988; Sas, 1993). Parental mental health problems are also consistently related to behavior problems in children (e.g., Essex, Klein, Miech, & Smider, 2001). Negative parent–child relationships and parental mental health problems are likely to be aspects of a broader level of family dysfunction that puts children at increased risk for maltreatment and poor mental health outcomes (Finkelhor, 1979; Haugaard & Reppucci, 1988;

Spaccarelli, 1994; Wolfe, Wolfe, & Best, 1988). Finally, low family SES, domestic violence, and parental criminal activity (Rutter & Quinton, 1977; Sameroff et al., 1993) further increase children's risk for adverse outcomes. In light of such associations, family-level factors must be considered as independent predictors of child victim/witnesses' long-term mental health. Also, although associations between family dysfunction and legal attitudes have not been previously examined, insofar as family dysfunction includes children's exposure to multiple kinds of maltreatment, parents' criminal activity, and parental mental health problems, higher levels of dysfunction may lead not only to mental health problems but to negative general attitudes about the legal system's fairness as well.

Additional Traumas

Regardless of CSA or legal involvement, greater exposure to stressors and adverse life events (e.g., living in out-of-home care, failing out of school, experiencing a severe illness) are associated with experiencing higher levels of mental health problems (e.g., Rutter & Quinton, 1977). Moreover, the occurrence of several such stressors is often not independent of CSA. For instance, compared with nonabused children, CSA victims are at increased risk for being revictimized; being placed in foster care, which may lead to being "bounced around" in the foster-care system (i.e., to experience multiple placements); and doing poorly in school (Arata, 2002; Tong, Oates, & McDowell, 1987; Widom, 1991). These stressors may relate to CSA victims' mental health and legal attitudes aside from their legal experiences. For example, repeated victimization is associated with poorer mental health (e.g., Arata, 2002). Also, Block et al. (2005) found that children involved in dependency court hearings (i.e., the juvenile court actions that determine if an abused child is placed in foster care) had more negative attitudes toward dependency court if their cases were also being heard in criminal court, suggesting that involvement in both systems concurrently adds to children's negative attitudes toward the legal system. To the extent that children's mental health and legal attitudes are adversely affected by life stressors, regardless of the children's specific experiences in the legal system, it is important to take into account such stressors when studying outcomes following child victim/witnesses' legal involvement.

Summary

In accordance with a multilevel-transactional approach, child and proximal factors must be considered when examining mental health and attitudinal outcomes following children's legal involvement. In addition to age, important child-level characteristics include gender and mental health before a legal case began. Being a female adolescent following exposure to CSA, for instance, is associated with increases in internalizing symptoms and more short-term negative attitudes toward the legal system (Goodman et al., 1992). Additionally, being more disturbed in childhood generally, before a prosecution even starts, is associated with mental health problems later on. Greater family risk, such as poor parental mental health, having been subjected to multiple forms of maltreatment, being exposed to domestic violence, and low family SES are also associated with poorer childhood and adult functioning. Finally, experiencing numerous adverse life events is a known risk factor for later psychopathology. By taking such factors into consideration, clearer insight into child victim/witnesses' later mental health and legal attitudes can be gained.

Further Considerations

From a scientific perspective, determining the impact of legal involvement separately from the impact of CSA, family dysfunction, and a host of other factors is challenging. As with virtually all research on CSA and legal involvement, one must be careful in drawing causal inferences because of complex interrelations among variables. For example, both CSA and family dysfunction can set children on particular developmental pathways that may be confounded with legal experience (e.g., Bagley, 1996; Kellogg, 2002; Reimer et al., 1996; Tebbutt, Swanston, Oates, & O'Toole, 1997). Moreover, an important cornerstone of scientific inference, random assignment to groups, is not realistic for this line of research. Our findings should be evaluated in light of these issues.

Our task is also made difficult by the fact that there is likely no single response to legal involvement, just as there is no single response to CSA (Kendell-Tackett et al., 1993; Masten & Wright, 1998). Not all maltreated children are affected by their experiences in the same way (known as "multifinality"; see Cicchetti & Rogosch, 1996). Moreover, CSA itself covers a host of experiences, from one-time sexualized kissing or exhibitionism to years of incest or prostitution. Similarly, legal involvement is different for each child, and specific legal experiences can vary widely across cases and jurisdictions. Thus, the absence of a single, clear response to legal involvement is to be expected. What is necessary, and what our study provides, is an investigation that takes into account multiple influences on children's outcomes, so that associations between legal involvement and psychological sequelae can be more clearly identified.

Furthermore, given the time period encompassed by our study, many years had passed between the children's legal involvement and our phone

19

call about the current research project. Many life changes undoubtedly occurred for study participants during the approximately 12-year interim. For example, since the completion of the Goodman et al. (1992) study, some of the children had progressed from being preschoolers to becoming older adolescents; others had progressed from adolescence into adulthood. Children's cognitive and socioemotional development presumably changed accordingly, for instance from representational levels of thought to more abstract reasoning (e.g., Fischer, 1980), or from the beginnings of abstract reasoning to the pragmatic, everyday problem solving of adulthood (e.g., LaBouvie-Vief, 1998). To answer some of our questions, the participants had to reconstruct experiences from memory, and do so from a new developmental perspective. Clearly, developmental change might influence how individuals react to their legal experiences over time.

Overall, then, many factors may make it difficult to detect simple, consistent patterns in victims' current responses. The outcomes of both CSA and legal involvement are likely to be varied. If consistent patterns in the long-term outcomes for the children are elusive, this would not be surprising. Alternatively, to the extent that consistent patterns do emerge, it is all the more remarkable, especially ones that rest largely on that single day—or those several days—when the child walked into the courtroom and testified.

HYPOTHESES

The overarching goal of our study was, from a developmental perspective, to understand the long-term psychological sequelae of legal involvement on CSA victim/witnesses. To do so, we considered children's ages when their legal involvement occurred, characteristics of their legal cases, and various other risk factors (e.g., adverse family experiences, CSA characteristics, and additional traumas and life stressors). Using a prospective-longitudinal design, we compared information collected at the time of children's original cases (i.e., on children's abuse and legal experiences, mental health, and emotional reactions at court) with information collected in the current study via interviews with the former victim/witnesses and their caregivers. We also interviewed a sample of matched control participants who had not experienced CSA or CSA-related legal involvement, and compared these individuals' functioning and attitudes with that of the former victim/witnesses.

Based on the literature reviewed, two sets of hypotheses were developed. One concerned predictors of current mental health, and the other concerned predictors of attitudes toward the legal system. Our main hypotheses focus on how age and legal experiences relate to the two sets of outcomes within the former victim/witnesses. However, we also developed several predictions concerning differences between the legal involvement sample (i.e., the former victim/witnesses) and the control sample (i.e., the individuals with no history of CSA or CSA-related legal involvement).

Mental Health Outcomes

Our first set of predictions concerned mental health outcomes in the legal involvement sample. Based on results of Goodman et al.'s (1992) study, testifying repeatedly was expected to predict poorer adjustment in the long term. Such a pattern was expected to be particularly robust among the subset of children who did not fare well in the short term and among children who were younger when they testified. We also hypothesized that testifying repeatedly in cases that involved particularly severe CSA would be associated with poorer adjustment. Severe CSA (e.g., that which involved a perpetrator who was a parent, sexual penetration) is associated with poorer adjustment. The stress of testifying likely exacerbates the adverse consequences already associated with severe CSA, leading to additive levels of adjustment problems that continue into adulthood. Although testifying was hypothesized to be related, overall, to poorer adjustment, in certain circumstances, not testifying was also expected to be related to poorer adjustment. One such circumstance concerned when the legal case resulted in a lenient sentence or not-guilty verdict. Individuals who did not have their day in court may later come to see not testifying as them not having had sufficient control or influence, especially if the defendant "walked" or received a lenient sentence. Another such circumstance pertains to less severe abuse. One's day in court might be more desired when the CSA was less traumatizing thus also potentially making the court experience less threatening.

Several other case characteristics were also expected to be associated with poorer functioning in the former victim/witnesses. This was hypothesized to be particularly likely when these characteristics were considered concurrently, as is accomplished in studies of cumulative and domain risk factors in developmental psychopathology (e.g., Deater-Deckard et al., 1998; Rutter & Quinton, 1972; Sameroff et al., 1993). Characteristics included taking part in repeated interviews, the case lacking corroborative evidence, the case involving multiple continuances, and children not receiving maternal support during the case (Goodman et al., 1992; Sas, 1993). Finally, being more upset at court (e.g., before testifying, while testifying) was expected to be associated with poorer adjustment in the long term. Similar findings were reported by Berliner and Conte (1995), who found that children's anxiety while waiting to testify predicted poorer functioning in the short term.

With regard to hypothesized differences in current functioning between the former victim/witnesses and individuals with no history of CSA, first, given the significance of adverse early trauma exposure on development and functioning (e.g., Edwards, Holden, Felitti, & Anda, 2003; Finkelhor, 1979; Marx & Sloan, 2003), CSA victims who were young when they were involved in the criminal prosecution and when they testified were expected to have the poorest levels of current adjustment. This especially poor adjustment is likely because of a number of factors, including being young when the CSA itself occurred, as well as young when exposed to the stress of legal involvement and of testifying (Runyan et al., 1988; Whitcomb et al., 1991). Second, consistent with research concerning risk factors and developmental psychopathology (e.g., see Cummings, Davis, & Campbell, 2000, for a review), the former victim/witnesses, especially those who testified, were expected to have more mental health problems than individuals with no CSA experiences. Third, across studies of children's reactions to adverse life events, females display more internalizing behavior problems, and males display more externalizing behavior problems (e.g., Leadbeater et al., 1999). We thus hypothesized that female victim/witnesses would report more internalizing symptoms (e.g., anxiety, somatic complaints, depression), and male victim/witnesses would report more externalizing symptoms.

Legal Attitude Outcomes

Our measures of individuals' attitudes toward the legal system included those concerning the CSA legal case in which the victim/witnesses had taken part (e.g., their satisfaction with the outcome) and those concerning feelings about the legal system generally (e.g., its fairness).

When considering the former CSA victim/witnesses, we first hypothesized those individuals who were older when the CSA legal case began would hold more negative feelings about their case specifically and about the legal system generally. With age, CSA victims are treated more harshly in the legal system; for instance, their credibility and motives are more likely to be questioned, and they are questioned in less supportive manners (Bottoms & Goodman, 1991; Goodman et al., 1992). Also with age, children's understanding of the seriousness of the legal case and its implications for them and their families improves (e.g., Block et al., 2005; Davis et al., 2005; Saywitz et al., 1989). Both of these factors should contribute to older individuals' more negative attitudes. Second, testifying repeatedly in a CSA case that involved especially severe abuse was expected to be associated with more negative current attitudes about the former case. This expectation is based on theorized additive adverse effects of multiple traumas—in this case, experiencing highly invasive abuse and then repeatedly testifying about what happened. Third, consistent with studies of child victims' perceptions of legal involvement in the short term (e.g., Goodman et al., 1992;

Sas, 1991), the outcome of the case was hypothesized to be strongly related to their attitudes: More lenient sentences would be associated with stronger negative feelings about the legal system's response to the former CSA case specifically but also about the legal system in general. This association was further expected to vary depending on whether individuals testified or not. Based on research suggesting that decision control is positively related to outcome satisfaction (Folger, 1977; Tyler, 1988) and consistent with the results of Goodman et al.'s (1992) original study, having not testified when the perpetrator received a lenient sentence (e.g., acquittal) was expected to be related to particularly negative current attitudes, about both the former case specifically and the legal system generally. Fourth, greater distress at court (e.g., while waiting and while on the witness stand) was expected to be related to more negative legal attitudes about the former case. Additionally, as mentioned, older children are treated more harshly when they are involved as victims in CSA legal cases (Goodman et al., 1992). Accordingly, former victim/witnesses who were older at the time of the legal case and also highly distressed at court (and hence who presumably were the most adversely affected by their harsh treatment) were expected to hold more negative legal attitudes than both individuals who were younger at the time of the case and individuals who were less distressed.

Our final set of predictions concerned attitudinal differences between the legal involvement sample and the nonabused control sample. We expected the former CSA victim/witnesses, regardless of whether they testified or not, to express more negativity toward the legal system (e.g., feeling that the system is unfair) than individuals with no CSA or CSA-related legal experiences. We further expected this group difference to be especially pronounced among older individuals and among female victim/witnesses, consistent with findings from short-term studies of attitudes in CSA victim/witnesses (Goodman et al., 1992; Sas, 1991).

II. METHOD

In this chapter, we first provide a précis of the Goodman et al. (1992) study on which the present project is based. We then move to a detailed discussion of the methods utilized in the current study, explaining how they were used to operationalize the ideas and test the hypotheses laid out at the end of Chapter I.

THE GOODMAN ET AL. (1992) STUDY

The goal of the 1992 study was to examine the short-term emotional effects of testifying in criminal court on sexually abused children. The 218 participants in the study varied in age from 4 to 17 years at the time of their court appearances and were quite diverse in race/ethnicity and SES. Sixty-one percent of the families who were eligible (i.e., those whose child was involved in prosecutions in three Colorado jurisdictions between 1985 and 1987) agreed to participate in the study. The child participants were generally representative of CSA victims whose cases were referred to the District Attorneys' Offices at that time. Specifically, participating families were comparable with nonparticipating families in: (a) race of the victim, (b) age, race, and gender of the defendant, (c) whether the child was injured and, if so, how severe the injury was, (d) abuse frequency, (e) official charge of incest, (f) whether a second type of offense was committed against the child (e.g., kidnapping, child physical abuse), and (g) type of sexual act (e.g., penetration vs. fondling). There was a slight tendency for the families of older female victims to decline participation, especially when the person accused of abuse was the girl's father or stepfather. Still, many such families participated (see Goodman et al., 1992, for details). Among the 218 participating children, 23% of the perpetrators were parents or stepparents, 43% of the perpetrators were nonparental persons in a position of trust (e.g., other family member, foster parent, mother's significant other), 27% of the perpetrators were acquaintances, and 6% of the perpetrators were strangers. Duration of abuse ranged from 1 day (44%), through periods ranging from 2 days to 6 months (31%), or more than 6 months to 5 years (22%), to over 5 years (3%). Type of abuse ranged from exhibitionism (1%), nongenital fondling (9%), or genital fondling/oral sex (48%), to vaginal or anal penetration (42%). Frequency of abuse ranged from 1 time (42%), through 2–3 times (21%), to 4 or more times (33%). There was 4% missing data. Most of the children were not injured (84%) but 16% suffered mild-to-moderate injury, and force was involved in 42% of the cases.

The general design of the 1992 study is presented in Table 1. Details can be obtained from the original SRCD *Monograph*, although several noteworthy characteristics are mentioned here because of their relevance to the current study. First, standardized measures of the children's behavioral adjustment and primary caretakers' mental health functioning were obtained shortly after the case was referred for prosecution. Nonoffending caregivers completed the Child Behavior Checklist (CBCL; Achenbach, 1994; Achenbach & Edelbrock, 1981), a measure of the child's behavioral adjustment in the previous month. They also completed the Social Adjustment Scale (SAS-R; Weissman & Bothwell, 1976), a measure of the parents' level of impairment in every day and social functioning (e.g., in interactions with spouse/

TABLE 1

EXPERIMENTAL DESIGN AND MEASURES USED IN THE GOODMAN ET AL. (1992) STUDY: THE TOTAL SAMPLE ($N = 218$) INCLUDES TESTIFIERS, MATCHED NONTESTIFIERS, AND ADDITIONAL NONTESTIFIERS

Intake ($N = 218$; case referred for prosecution; home visit); Informed consent (parent and child); Sexual Assault Profile (Conte & Berliner, 1984; DAs' files, primary caretaker, and child testimony); details concerning abuse (e.g., corroborative evidence, demographics, child's coping, maternal support, relationship to defendant, placement out of home, etc.); Achenbach Child Behavior Checklist (CBCL; primary caretaker report of child's behavioral disturbance); Social Adjustment Scale (SAS; caretaker self report of own social functioning)

Precourt ($N = 110$; court building while child waiting to see if need to testify); Spielberger State Anxiety Scale; Before Court Measure (child's feelings about having to testify); Abbreviated form of CBCL (parent report of child distress in last 48 hours)

Court—Testifiers only ($N = 60$); court observations (ratings of child during testimony and court members' behaviors)

Postcourt—Testifiers only; Post Court Measure (child's feelings about having testified)

Follow-up; 3 months post-testimony (Testifiers and Nontestifier Matches); Achenbach CBCL

Follow-up; 7 months post-testimony (Testifiers and Nontestifier Matches); Achenbach CBCL

Follow-up; final post-testimony (Testifiers and Nontestifier Matches); Achenbach CBCL

Other measures: Case Progress (facts concerning case progress through the legal system, $N = 218$); Legal Involvement Questionnaires, parent ($N = 113$) and child ($N = 72$) versions (parent's and child's reactions to experiences in the legal system).

romantic partner, children); such impairment correlates with poor mental health. The CBCL and SAS-R provide a baseline for child and parent mental health problems at the start of the prosecution for use in the current study of long-term correlates of legal involvement.

Second, detailed descriptions of the abuse (e.g., duration, perpetrator–child relationship, sexual acts), investigation (e.g., number of interviews), and prosecution (e.g., length of legal involvement, testimony at trial, case outcome) were obtained from District Attorney files, questionnaires filled out by or completed during interviews with children's caretakers, and/or observations of courtroom testimony. Because the children were involved in active prosecutions, Goodman et al. were not permitted to question them directly about their abuse experiences. None of the jurisdictions in which data collection took place had formal court preparation programs in place. Nor did they systematically use special accommodations to enhance children's ability to provide accurate and complete testimony (e.g., closed-circuit television or barriers or shields in the courtroom). On an individual basis, some children were provided with tours of the court before they testified (e.g., by a victim advocate). However, these tours were brief and often occurred on the same day that children actually testified. Also, for some children, a victim advocate was allowed to stand near children while they testified to provide support. Such procedures are described in detail in the 1992 *Monograph*.

Third, those children who went to the courthouse expecting to testify, even if they did not testify, for instance because of a last-minute plea bargain, were interviewed while they were waiting. Questions concerned their anxiety (e.g., using the Spielberger State Anxiety Scale) and feelings about taking the stand. For instance, children were asked to rate how they felt about being at court, talking to the judge, seeing their attorney, and seeing the defendant. Ratings were made on a four-point face scale that ranged from a face with a large smile to a face with a large frown. (Similar questions were administered to children who took the stand after they finished testifying.)

Fourth, for the subset of children who actually testified (either at a hearing or trial), researchers observed the children during their testimony and documented their reactions and experiences (e.g., by rating on five-point scales how happy/sad children were at proscribed times, by rating whether children cried while testifying). None of the children testified in concurrent dependency hearings resulting from the CSA (i.e., hearings in juvenile court to decide whether the children should be removed from an unsafe home environment). Also, in most cases, the main reason why children did not testify was that the defendant accepted a plea bargain. Other reasons why children did not testify included that the defendant was still at large, the case was dismissed, or the case was still ongoing when the original study ended. All cases have since ended.

Fifth, the child victims who testified and a matched group of victims who did not testify were followed throughout the criminal court process. The groups were matched on such key variables as behavioral adjustment at the start of the prosecution (i.e., CBCL total T score), abuse severity, age, gender, race/ethnicity, SES, and relationship to the accused. Post-legal involvement questionnaires administered to the two groups concerned the children's behavioral adjustment (i.e., the CBCL was recompleted 3 and 7 months post-testimony and after the case closed) and both the children's and their caretakers' reactions to the legal system (e.g., on four-point scales assessing fairness of the legal process, satisfaction with the case outcome, effects of the case on their lives, and effects of not testifying).

PRESENT STUDY OVERVIEW

For the present research, we reinterviewed participants from the prior study, years after that study ended. We also added a group of children living in a similar area with no known history of CSA (i.e., "control group") that matched as closely as possible the victim/witness participants in the 1992 study in terms of age, gender, SES, race/ethnicity, and behavioral adjustment as indexed by CBCL scores obtained in the 1980s. Because the CBCL, the measure of behavioral adjustment for children at the start of the prosecution in the 1992 study, was also available for the control group, we were able to control statistically for initial behavior problems, facilitating comparisons in the groups' later mental health and legal attitudes. The control group differed from the legal involvement group in two ways (i.e., child sexual victimization and legal involvement). However, within the legal involvement group, there was considerable variability in the extent of the former victim/witnesses' actual participation in the case. That is, many of the children from the legal involvement sample had only limited interactions with the legal system concerning the CSA (e.g., a single interview with a police officer, after which the defendant confessed and a plea bargain was arranged), despite the fact that their case was referred for prosecution. Therefore, a continuum existed from the control group participants (who had no known CSA or legal involvement) to CSA victims with virtually no legal involvement to CSA victims with considerable legal involvement. Details concerning the comparability of the different subsamples in the current study (legal involvement participants who testified in their case or "testifiers," legal involvement participants who had not testified or "nontestifiers," and the controls) will be presented in Chapter III.

The final outcomes of all 218 cases, which were not fully known at the close of the 1992 Goodman et al. study, were known at the time of the present study. A majority of the cases ($n = 164$) ended in a plea bargain. Ten

27

cases were dismissed because of lack of probable cause or evidence, and 12 cases were dismissed because of a technicality or because the child did not testify (e.g., the District Attorney's office was prosecuting the defendant in a separate stronger case, the child refused to testify, the child was too emotionally fragile to testify and was deemed "unavailable" as a witness). Of the 32 cases that went to trial, 21 ended in a guilty verdict (with one being overturned later on appeal) and 11 ended in acquittals.

Finally, for all cases that were still in progress when the original study ended ($n = 49$), we obtained court documentation to determine the case outcome and learn whether or not the original study participant testified after the completion of the 1992 study. Two young adults who had not testified by the end of the original study testified later. Thus, although classified as nontestifiers in the 1992 study, these two individuals were reclassified as testifiers in the present study.

Research Plan

In the current study, individuals completed a phone interview (Phase 1), followed by a set of mailed questionnaires (Phase 2). Although there was some attrition (see Tables 2 and 3), both phases were completed by: (a) individuals who began their legal cases approximately $12 \frac{1}{2}$ years previously (the *legal involvement group*), (b) individuals in the *control group* (added for the present study), and (c) both groups' primary nonoffending caregivers. Phase 1 questions concerned participants' personal, family, victimization, and delinquency/crime histories; mental health functioning; and current perceptions of the legal system. Conducting Phase 1 via telephone optimized the opportunity to collect data from all located participants, but this phase had to be relatively brief (approximately 30 minutes). Phase 2 was designed to obtain additional information about participants' mental health and victimization/legal history.

For both ethical and scientific reasons, we did not tell participants that we knew of their past victimization histories or that they had participated in our earlier research. If participants did not remember the documented CSA (e.g., because they were too young at the time it happened), an unfamiliar interviewer calling unexpectedly and informing them of their past abuse could cause considerable distress. Moreover, from a scientific standpoint, it was better for the interviewers to be blind to study hypotheses and the participants' prior experiences. That is, because we were testing hypotheses concerning long-term outcomes following CSA and legal involvement, it was important for interviewers to know as little as possible, in advance, of the details concerning individual participants' experiences, because this might have affected how they asked questions or decided how to follow-up on participants' responses.

28

TABLE 2

ADOLESCENT AND YOUNG ADULT RESPONSE RATES FOR PHASES 1 AND 2 OF THE PRESENT
STUDY

| | Adolescent and Young Adult Group | | |
Participation Status	Target	Control	Total
Phase 1			
Total initially eligible	218	58	276
Deceased	1	0	1
Unlocatable	33	10	43
Invited to participate	184	48	232
Refused	9	1	10
Participated	175	47	222
Cases excluded	1	6	7
Total participants	*174*	*41*	*215*
Phase 2			
Total initially eligible	174	41	215
Unlocatable[a]	36	9	45
Invited to participate	138	32	170
Refused	9	0	9
Participated	129	32	161
Total participants	*129*	*32*	*161*

Note.—[a]Participants who never responded to the Phase 2 mailed questionnaires are classified as "un-locatable." It is possible that some of these individuals did not wish to complete the second phase and simply elected not to respond to our requests. However, we did not know whether they received the questionnaires. Hence they are included with unlocatable participants.

Participants were initially contacted and asked to take part in a study concerning attitudes and experiences with the legal system. Most participants had to be called more than once (e.g., no one was home when they were called the first time or they were home but did not have time to talk). When answering machines were available, interviewers left messages along with a toll-free number that individuals could call to learn more about the study. Once participants were contacted, they were informed that their names were obtained from lists of individuals and families who had previously taken part in research concerning family functioning, life experiences, and child development, or because their family visited a public or private family resource center (which had occurred for some control participants). Although rare, participants who queried further were told that the interviewer did not have any documentation regarding from which of the aforementioned sources individual participants' names were obtained, but that the participants could call the researchers at a toll-free number to find out more. None of the participants called. Participants were also informed that the phone interview would take approximately 30 to 45

TABLE 3

CAREGIVER RESPONSE RATES FOR PHASES 1 AND 2 OF THE PRESENT STUDY

| | Caregiver Group | | |
Participation Status	Target	Control	Totals
Phase 1			
Total initially eligible	200	58	258
Deceased	5	1	6
Unlocatable	40	12	52
Invited to participate	155	45	200
Refused	17	0	17
Participated	138	45	183
Cases excluded	0	6	6
Total participants	*138*	*39*	*177*
Phase 2			
Total initially eligible	138	39	177
Unlocatable[a]	29	2	31
Invited to participate	109	37	146
Refused	12	3	15
Participated	97	34	131
Total participants	*97*	*34*	*131*

Note.—[a]Caregivers who never responded to the Phase 2 mailed questionnaires are classified as "unlocatable." It is possible that some of these individuals did not wish to complete the second phase and simply elected not to respond to our requests. However, we did not know whether they received the questionnaires. Hence they are included with unlocatable Phase 2 caregivers.

minutes, depending on their life experiences which often prompted participants to reschedule interviews or ask the interviewer to call at a different time.

At the beginning of each study phase, verbal or written consent was secured. For adolescent participants younger than age 18 years, caregivers' consent for their child's participation was obtained prior to approaching the adolescent about the study. During the consent procedures, participants were informed about the sensitive nature of some interview questions and that they should be in a place where they would feel comfortable answering the questions. They were also told they could skip questions or end the entire interview at any point. Participants were further assured confidentiality of their responses, except in situations where they provided information that suggested they or someone else may be in current danger of being harmed. Phone interviews were conducted by highly trained female interviewers from the National Opinion Research Center (NORC) at the University of Chicago or by highly trained female researchers at the University of California, Davis (UC Davis). All interviewers were trained to conduct sensitive interviews and had begun the interviews blind to study hypotheses and participant group status, except in a small number of cases. These exceptions occurred when particular individuals proved especially difficult to locate, in which cases the lead researchers made vigorous efforts to find, contact, and interview the individuals in question. Even under such circumstances, the researchers were blind to specific details of individual participants' prior abuse and legal experiences (e.g., whether or not the individual had testified).

After each phase of the study, participants were paid and sent a letter thanking them for participating. Included in the letter was a toll-free number they could call if they had questions or concerns about the study. A debriefing letter was also sent once participants had completed the final phase of the study. The letter described the general goals and importance of the study (e.g., to examine legal attitudes and legal involvement), again without indicating knowledge of the participants' past history. The debriefing statement also contained a toll-free number to call if participants were concerned about any of the questions (we had contact information for local clinicians and mental health clinics if the need arose for a referral). All study procedures were approved by the Human Subjects Review Committees at UC Davis and the University of Denver (two universities that oversaw subject recruitment and participation), and a Certificate of Confidentiality was obtained from the National Institutes of Health.

PARTICIPANTS

For purposes of clarity, *"target adolescents and young adults"* refers to the child participants in Goodman et al.'s (1992) legal involvement sample, who were adolescents and young adults at the time of the present study. *"Control adolescents and young adults"* refers to participants with no known history of CSA or CSA-related legal involvement.

Target Adolescents and Young Adults

A total of 218 target children participated in the 1992 study. Following that study, one participant died and another was determined to have experienced sexual assault that did not meet the legal definition of CSA (the perpetrator was not quite 4 years older than the child), causing both people to be left out of the present study. Of the remaining 216 potential target adolescents and young adults, 174 (81%), including 140 females and 34 males, completed Phase 1. Their ages at the time of Phase 1 ranged from 16.67 to 30.33 ($M = 23$ years). Detailed information regarding the numbers of individuals who completed both phases, who refused to participate, and who were unlocatable is presented in Table 2. Demographic characteristics

31

of the sample are described in the preliminary analyses (Chapter III). No significant differences emerged between target adolescents and young adults who took part in the present study and those who did not take part in the present study with respect to age when the abuse began and ended, abuse characteristics (e.g., type of sexual contact, relationship to perpetrator, number of abuse experiences), or legal experiences (e.g., number of times testified), t's ≤ 1.60, df's 199–216. Females were more likely than males to agree to take part in the research, $\chi^2(1) = 7.14$, $p < .01$, although the proportion of females and males in the current study nonetheless mirrors that found in national prevalence reports of CSA (e.g., U.S. Department of Health and Human Services, 2002).

Control Adolescents and Young Adults

The control adolescents and young adults included children with no known history of CSA. This sample was solicited from two main sources: (a) child participants who had taken part in various other studies conducted by Goodman and colleagues at the time of the 1992 study and who had been assessed with the CBCL at that time (i.e., 1986–1988; some of the children had been matched in the 1980s to a subset of the CSA victims; Goodman, Bottoms, Rudy, Davis, & Schwartz-Kenney, 2001), and (b) children who had visited a mental health clinic in the Denver area and for whom the CBCL had been completed during the same time period when the 1992 study took place. Demographic information (e.g., parents' occupation, children's ethnicity, children's age) and CBCL scores were available for all control participants. For clinic patients, names of young adults and adolescents whose CBCL scores and ages were within the range of the legal involvement sample were identified in clinic records by clinic staff (i.e., not the present study's researchers). A letter was sent from the clinic about the study, along with a response card that the person could return directly to us if she/he was interested in hearing more about the present study. Those who returned the response card were contacted and invited to take part. Across both sample-recruitment strategies, 58 possible control participants were identified. Forty-seven individuals (81%) took part in Phase 1 (see Table 2 for response-rate details; see Chapter III for demographic characteristics and preliminary analyses). During the course of the study, in which individuals were provided with definitions of CSA and asked if they had experienced such actions, six control individuals indicated that they had previously been victims of CSA. They were thus eliminated from the study, leaving 41 control adults and adolescents in the final sample, 15 males and 26 females, ages 15.92–26.77 ($M = 19.58$ years).

It is possible that a few of the control participants included in the final sample had also experienced CSA. For example, they might not have remembered their prior experiences. Or they or their caregivers might not have elected, during their participation in the current study, to report the incidents. Regardless of the reason, this possibility would likely increase the similarity between the legal involvement and control groups (because some of the latter experienced CSA), thereby reducing our ability to identify effects of legal involvement following child sexual victimization. Thus, our findings may be somewhat conservative.

Caregivers

Of the 200 target caregivers who took part in the Goodman et al. (1992) study, 17 had more than one child in the study. One hundred and thirty-six (68%) of these caregivers participated in the present study, including 13 caregivers of two children and one caregiver of three children. Some caregivers had died, or were foster parents or other nonparental caregivers who were not in contact with the adolescents or young adults at the time of the current study. For these cases, alternate caregivers (e.g., another family member who was currently in contact with the participant, excluding the former perpetrator) were administered questionnaires regarding the adolescents' or young adults' current well-being. For the control participants, 58 caregivers were eligible, and 45 completed Phase 1. Caregivers of the six young adults in the control group who reported CSA were excluded from the final sample. Caregiver response rates are presented in Table 3.

QUESTIONNAIRES

The study questionnaires were designed to cover a range of victimization experiences and legal contact. Questions not of direct relevance to the present report are described only briefly here to provide insight into the overall methodology and participants' experiences during the study. Table 4 lists the primary dependent measures of interest here, along with the phase during which they were completed and by whom.

Adolescent and Young Adult Phase 1 Questionnaires

The possibility that we would be unable to locate or interview respondents more than once motivated us to design the Phase 1 interview so that it covered a range of issues, especially for the adolescent and young adult participants, within the relatively brief time frame afforded by a phone interview. Questions were generally asked in the order presented below, with minor exceptions in a few instances.

33

TABLE 4

PRIMARY DEPENDENT MEASURES OF INTEREST IN THE PRESENT STUDY

Study Phase	Measure of Interest
Phase 1	
Mental health	Subset of Brief Symptoms Inventory (BSI) Items[a]
Legal attitudes	Perceptions of the fairness of the legal system[a]
	Perceptions of the treatment of victims and defendants in court[a]
	Ratings of the effects of the target case on individuals' lives[b]
	Satisfaction with the original target case outcome[b]
	Ratings of the effects of testifying on individuals' lives[b]
	Ratings of the effects of not testifying on individuals' lives[b]
Phase 2	
Mental health	Trauma Symptoms Inventory (TSI)[a]
	Post-Traumatic Stress Diagnostic Scale (PDS)[a]
	Dissociative Experiences Scale (DES)[a]
	Young Adult Self Report Behavior Checklist (YASR)[a]
	Young Adult Behavior Checklist (YABCL)[c]

Notes. — [a]Measures completed by the adolescent and young adult participants.
[b]Measures completed by subsets of legal involvement participants, depending on their disclosures of the former CSA legal case and reports of testifying or not.
[c]Measure completed by caregivers.

Demographic Questions

The demographic questions concerned age, residence in Colorado during the mid-1980s, employment, education, marital status, and number of children.

Brief Symptom Inventory (BSI)

The BSI is a well-established measure of psychopathology, standardized for use with adolescents and adults (Derogatis & Lazarus, 1994; Derogatis & Melisaratos, 1983). Alpha coefficients range from .71 to .85 across the BSI subscales (e.g., depression, anxiety). The BSI also has excellent test–retest reliability, with stability coefficients of approximately .90 (Croog, Levine, Testa, Brown, Bulpitt, Jenkins, Klerman, & Williams, 1986; Derogatis, 1993). Respondents rate how frequently (from $1 =$ never to $5 =$ extremely) they have been distressed by various problems during the last 7 days. Nine items were included (i.e., feeling fearful, feeling that most people cannot be trusted, feeling tense or keyed up, feeling worthlessness, having trouble catching one's breath, feeling lonely, exhibiting temper outbursts they could not control, feeling uneasy in crowds, and having trouble remembering things). These items correspond to those with the highest factor loadings on each of nine BSI subscales (Derogatis & Melisaratos, 1983).

General Legal Attitudes

These questions, designed for the present study, required respondents to rate their agreement, using a four-point scale (1 = strongly agree, 4 = strongly disagree), with statements concerning the harshness of the legal system's treatment of victims of crime and of people accused of crime (e.g., "The U.S. Criminal Courts are too harsh on victims of crimes"). Additional questions required respondents to rate the fairness, on a four-point scale (1 = very fair, 4 = very unfair), of police practices, criminal courts, and juvenile courts (e.g., "How would you rate the fairness, overall, of the criminal courts in the U.S.?").

Legal and Victimization Experiences

These questions, also devised for the present study, concerned several topics. The *Legal Experiences* questions asked the number of times (if any) respondents experienced: (a) robbery, (b) burglary, (c) sexual offenses as an adult, (d) sexual assault as a child or adolescent, (e) physical assault as a child, adolescent, or adult, and (f) other crimes. For example, the question about robbery was, "Robbery is when someone physically forces or threatens to force you to give them something of yours. How many times have you ever, including as a child or adult, been the victim of robbery?" Response options included "never," "1 time," "2–3 times," "4–5 times," "6–9 times," or "more than 10 times." Respondents who had experienced any of these crimes were asked how many of them had been reported to the authorities, and, for those that had not been reported, the reasons why. Participants who indicated that one of the crimes had been reported to authorities were asked to "Rate the effects of the police investigations and/or criminal prosecutions on your life" on a four-point scale (1 = very positive to 4 = very negative) and to "Rate your satisfaction with the legal system's responses" on a four-point scale (1 = very satisfied to 4 = very unsatisfied). Participants who indicated that they had experienced CSA that was reported to the authorities were asked the defendant's name; whether they were involved in a criminal prosecution, social service investigation, or juvenile court action; the year the court action took place; and the main negative and positive consequences of the legal involvement, either in the short term or in the long term. CSA was defined as exhibitionism, sexual touching, rape, oral sex, penetration, intercourse, or any other type of sexual assault (completed or

35

attempted acts) that occurred before age 18 and with a person more than 4 years older (see Alexander, Quas, Goodman, Ghetti, Edelstein, Redlich, Cordon, & Jones, 2005).

False Report questions concerned whether, for any of the crimes discussed previously, the respondent had been involved in a false report, and if so, which crime was falsely reported and how old the respondent was at the time. These questions were included, for instance, to discriminate individuals who did not remember the former documented CSA case from individuals who might say they were not abused because in their minds, the CSA was a false report.

Testifying questions concerned whether respondents had ever testified in court, and if so, their age, the reason for testifying, and the type of court (juvenile vs. criminal). Respondents were also asked if they ever, as a crime victim, wanted to testify but did not get to or did not want to testify and did not have to. These questions were followed by probes concerning the respondents' age at the time, type of court, and feelings (e.g., wanted to testify, mixed feelings). Finally, respondents who assented to either of the above questions (about having testified or not) were asked to rate the effects of testifying or not testifying, respectively, on their lives (1 = very positive, 4 = very negative; e.g., "For each crime you mentioned, how would you rate the effect, overall, of NOT testifying on your life?"). These questions paralleled those asked in the original Goodman et al. (1992) study.

A series of *Victimization* questions concerned participants' prior victimization experiences, regardless of whether these experiences were reported to the authorities. A primary purpose of these questions was to identify whether target participants disclosed the documented CSA case (for details on disclosure, see Goodman, Ghetti, Ques, Alexander, Redlich, Cordon, & Jones, 2003). A second purpose was to assess the frequency of abuse and other childhood and adult victimization experiences.

Questions about CSA concerned whether participants experienced CSA and the number of CSA occurrences with different perpetrators, defined as separate instances with different individuals (e.g., repeated incest with a stepfather, a single sexual assault by a stranger, and gang rape were each considered a single occurrence; sexual abuse by a father and later by a neighbor were counted as two occurrences). For each reported occurrence, follow-up questions asked about the perpetrator's gender and relationship to the respondent, the respondent's age when each experience began and ended, the frequency of the abuse (i.e., 1 time, 2–3 times, 4–5 times, 6–9 times, 10–15 times, 16–20 times, over 20 times), type of contact (e.g., fondling, penetration), whether the perpetrator was reported to the authorities, the outcome of the report, and the consequences of the assault on their life (e.g., family arguments increased, nervousness or anxiety, illness, and/or pregnancy). Additionally, for each occurrence that was reported to the authorities, participants were asked, "How satisfied are you with the legal outcome of the case?" (response options ranged from 1 = very satisfied to 4 = very unsatisfied) and "What was the effect, overall, of the police investigation and/or criminal prosecution on your life?" (response options ranged from 1 = very positive to 4 = very negative). The latter two questions paralleled those asked in Goodman et al.'s (1992) study.

A final set of questions pertained to whether the respondents had ever forgotten the CSA experiences. Results relevant to these questions are reported separately (see Ghetti, Edelstein, Goodman, Cordon, Quas, Alexander, Redlich, & Jones, in press). A virtually identical set of questions as those asked about CSA was asked about child physical abuse (CPA). The CSA and CPA questions were counterbalanced: some participants were asked about CPA first, and others were asked about CSA first. No significant differences were observed regarding the number of perpetrators or the frequency of maltreatment based on question order, and thus order is not considered further.

Other victimization questions concerned whether, during childhood, the respondent had witnessed domestic violence between her/his primary caregivers or had been a victim of emotional abuse or physical neglect. Respondents were also asked whether any of these incidents were reported to the authorities and, if so, the outcome of the report. Finally, respondents 18 years of age and older were asked about experiences of sexual assault and domestic violence as an adult, with follow-up questions asking about their relationship to the perpetrator of each incident and whether any of the experiences were reported to the authorities.

For each type of victimization, if respondents said they had never experienced such acts, they were asked, "Did you really not experience it, or did you experience it but you don't want to talk about it?" If a respondent indicated the latter, he/she was assured that no more questions on the topic would be asked. Across the victimization questions, the percentage of individuals who indicated that they did not want to talk about a particular topic ranged from 1% for witnessing domestic violence to 4% for experiences of CPA; CSA (3%) fell between the two.

Additional Legal Involvement questions concerned the respondent's experiences with the legal system as an alleged perpetrator. These included whether the respondent had been convicted of committing any crime, convicted of committing a felony, or suspected by legal or social services authorities of child maltreatment.

Trauma questions (scored as "yes" or "no") included whether the respondent had ever been abandoned by one or both parents, lived in a group or foster home, experienced other negative life experiences (e.g., death of a loved one, parental divorce, an alcoholic or drug-addicted parent, failing out of school, an abusive sibling), or had parents who were jailed.

A final set of questions concerned whether participants had been in therapy, their current contact with the nonoffending caregiver who participated in the 1992 study (respondents were told only that we had that person's name listed from previous records; nothing was said about the prior study); their closeness while growing up to their biological mother and father (1 = not very close; 5 = very close); and whether there was another adult in their childhood to whom they felt emotionally close (yes–no). These final questions helped us determine whether the target caregiver was appropriate to complete questionnaires regarding participants' functioning.

Adolescent and Young Adult Phase 2 Questionnaires

The Phase 2 questionnaires concerned participants' mental health, victimization and legal experiences, legal attitudes about certain types of victims, criminal and delinquent behavior, and risk of alcoholism. Phase 2 dependent measures of interest in the current report are presented in Table 4.

Mental Health Questionnaires

Several standardized measures of adolescents' and young adults' behavioral adjustment were included. The *Young Adult Self-Report* (YASR, Achenbach, 1997) is a measure of self-reported behavior problems. The measure is similar to Achenbach's CBCL, but is based on self- rather than caregiver-report and is standardized for use with 18–30-year olds. Participants rate whether behaviors (e.g., having trouble keeping friends, setting fires, being shy or timid) are not true, somewhat true, or very true of themselves. The YASR provides age- and gender-normative scores for overall adjustment, internalizing behavior problems (e.g., depression, anxiety), and externalizing behavior problems (e.g., aggression, delinquency). Higher scores reflect poorer adjustment. The reliability and validity of the measure have been extensively documented. For example, 1-week test–retest reliability (r) is .89 for total behavior problems (e.g., Achenbach, 1997, 1999).

The *Trauma Symptoms Inventory* (TSI; Briere, Elliot, Harris, & Cotman, 1995) is a measure of several kinds of trauma-related behavior problems (e.g., defensive avoidance, sexual concerns). Participants rate, on a four-point scale (0 = never to 3 = often), how often they have experienced various symptoms during the past six months. Responses are combined into subscales. Of special interest in the present study were the following subscales: sexual concerns (e.g., "Confusion about your sexual feelings"), sexual dysfunction (e.g., "Using sex to feel powerful or important"), defensive avoidance (e.g., "Trying to forget a bad time in your life"), and post-traumatic symptoms (e.g., "Sudden disturbing memories when you were not expecting them"). On each subscale, higher scores indicate more problems. The reliability of these subscales has been demonstrated in both clinical and nonclinical samples, with α coefficients ranging from .84 to .86 across subscales (Briere et al., 1995; Smiljanich & Briere, 1993). Scores also reliably distinguish individuals who have experienced various childhood and adult stressors, including CSA, from those with no such experiences (Briere et al., 1995).

A second measure that tapped post-traumatic stress symptomatology was the *Post-Traumatic Diagnostic Scale* (PDS; Foa, Cashman, Jaycox, & Perry, 1997). This measure has been validated with clinical interviews and other self-report trauma measures in individuals who have experienced a wide range of trauma experiences (e.g., victims of natural disasters, assaults, war). It provides a categorical diagnosis of post-traumatic stress disorder (PTSD) as well as an index of symptom severity. The PDS has high internal consistency, good test–retest reliability, and strong associations with structured interview assessments of PTSD. For instance, coefficient α for symptom severity is .92, and, in terms of classification capability, sensitivity is .89 and specificity is .75 (Foa et al., 1997).

The *Dissociative Experiences Scale* (DES; Bernstein & Putnam, 1986) assesses the frequency of dissociative experiences, ranging from normal to pathological, and has been widely used in research with adults and adolescents. Participants indicate on a scale from 0% to 100% how frequently they have had various experiences (e.g., "Some people have the experience of finding new things among their belongings that they do not remember buying"). Higher scores indicate greater dissociative tendencies. The measure has good test–retest reliability (e.g., coefficient α's range from .92 to .95 across the DES subscales), internal consistency, and discriminant validity for dissociative disorder diagnoses (Bernstein & Putnam, 1986). Additionally, α coefficients for total DES scores are above .96 across repeated administrations (Dubester & Braun, 1995).

Additional Phase 2 Questions

In addition to the aforementioned measures, several other questions and questionnaires were included. For instance, closed-ended questions were asked about participants' contact with the legal system as defendants (i.e., whether participants had ever been arrested or jailed, scored dichotomously). A measure of delinquent behavior, adapted from the National Youth Survey (Elliott & Ageton, 1980; Huizinga & Elliot, 1983) asked about the frequency with which participants had engaged in various delinquent acts as adolescents. Other questions concerned perceptions of the fairness of the legal system to victims of CSA, CPA, and domestic violence. The Short-Form of the Michigan Alcohol Screening Test (SMAST; Seltzer, Vinokur, & Van Rooijen, 1975) and a measure of adult romantic attachment, the Close Relationships Questionnaire (Bartholomew & Horowitz, 1991), were also administered. None of these measures is considered further here, although several findings associated with these measures are described in other publications and presentations based on this study (e.g., Alexander et al., 2005; Goodman et al., 2003; Edelstein, Ghetti, Quas, Goodman, Alexander, Redlich, & Cordon, in press; Redlich, Alexander, Goodman, Quas, Ghetti, & Edelstein, 2000).

Caregiver Questionnaires

The adolescents' and young adults' caregivers also completed questionnaires in Phases 1 and 2. However, only a minority of the caregivers' responses, specifically those concerning the young adults' current mental health, is relevant to the present report. These responses pertain to the *Young Adult Behavior Checklist* (YABCL, Achenbach, 1997), a measure of the adolescents' and young adult participants' current behavioral adjustment, completed by caregivers in Phase 2. The YABCL is a psychometrically sound upward extension of the CBCL, completed by parents (or other caregivers, observers, etc.) of 18–30-year-olds. It correlates well with the CBCL and provides age- and gender-normed indices of internalizing and externalizing problems and an overall behavioral adjustment score (Achenbach, 1999). Reliability and validity of the YABCL are well documented. For instance, test–retest reliability is high, with $r = .87$ for total behavior problems. Also, the correlation between parents is .63 for total behavior problems. Higher YABCL scores indicate poorer adjustment.

PROCEDURE

Locating Participants

Numerous methods were employed in the study to locate the target legal involvement adolescents and young adults, the control group adolescents and young adults, and the caregivers. First, families from the 1992 study had provided names and contact information for individuals who would always know their whereabouts. This contact information allowed us to locate many of the target participants. Second, names and birthdates were available for all legal involvement and control participants and many former caregivers. From this information, public database searches were conducted, such as Department of Motor Vehicle record searches, property searches, credit record checks, and official criminal record searches. By using these techniques, we were able to locate 84% of the target adolescents and young adults and 80% of their caregivers (see Tables 2 and 3 for details).

Phase 1

Once a potential participant was located, she/he was invited to take part in a survey concerning attitudes about and experiences with the legal system. Young adults' identities were confirmed by verifying their name, date of birth, and residence in Colorado in the 1980s. Caregivers' identities were similarly confirmed, as was their relationship to the young adult. A few former foster-parent caregivers did not recognize the adolescent's or young adult's name, but confirmed that they were a foster parent living in the correct residential area during the 1980s. These individuals were only asked demographic questions and other specific questions regarding their experiences with and attitudes toward the legal system.

After individuals' identities were confirmed, the interviewer then read a consent script describing the study procedures, the potential risks and benefits of participation, and confidentiality of participants' responses. The researcher noted two exceptions to confidentiality: (a) if participants informed the interviewer that either they or someone else was in danger, and (b) if a new incident of child abuse was disclosed (i.e., an incident never reported to the authorities) that indicated a minor was currently at risk of being harmed. In either of these situations, the interviewer was to report this information to the authorities. (In the study, no reports of danger to the self or others, including no new reports of abuse risk for minors, were made.)

After being fully informed about the study, participants were asked if they had time to answer questions in a private location. If so, they were asked to give their verbal consent to participate (and/or give assent for their minor child to be interviewed), and the interview commenced. The mean delay between Time 1 (which corresponds to when caregivers completed the CBCL, which was at the start of the legal case for the target participants) and Phase 1 ranged from 10.33 to 16.17 years ($M = 12.62$, $SD = 1.10$) (see Chapter III, Table 5, for the breakdown by testify status: testifiers, non-testifiers, and controls).

A majority of adolescents and young adults (88%; 152 targets and 38 controls) and caretakers (95%; 128 targets and 38 controls) completed Phase 1 via phone. However, 10% of the young adults and adolescents (19 targets and three controls), and 4% of the caretakers (six targets and one control) elected to complete it via mail, and 1.4% of the young adults and adolescents (three targets) and 1% of the caregivers (two targets) completed it during an in-person meeting. No significant differences emerged across any of the dependent measures in the current study based on the method of completing the Phase 1 interview.

Two significant differences emerged between participants located and interviewed by the NORC interviewers (65%) and those located and interviewed by the UC Davis interviewers (35%). Compared with UC Davis-interviewed participants, NORC-interviewed participants were better functioning according to the mean of the nine items from the Brief Symptoms Inventory asked in Phase 1, $t(211) = 2.34$, $p < .05$. Also, among the target participants who disclosed the documented CSA case in Phase 1, those interviewed by NORC rated the effects of the CSA legal case on their lives as less negative than did those interviewed by UC Davis researchers, $t(112) = -2.46$, $p < .05$. It is important to understand that the UC Davis research team located and interviewed individuals who were unlocatable by NORC. It is likely that individuals who have poorer mental health are more difficult to find, leading to the evident differences based on interviewer group. Such an interpretation is supported by differences in participants' behavioral adjustment CBCL total T scores completed during the 1992 study and during the Phase 2 questionnaires in the current study, which were completed by mail. That is, participants who were questioned by the NORC interviewers in Phase 1 had significantly lower original CBCL T scores, $M = 59.75$ (better behavioral adjustment scores), than did participants questioned by the UC Davis researchers, $M = 66.04$, $t(189) = 3.76$, $p < .001$. During Phase 2, the participants who had been interviewed during Phase 1 by NORC reported lower scores on the DES (indicating fewer dissociative symptoms) than did the UC Davis-interviewed participants, $t(134) = 2.48$, $p < .05$. Because neither the 1992 study nor Phase 2 questionnaires (which were mailed) involved the NORC or UC Davis interviewers, the differences were not a result of interviewer practices. Moreover, for most of the Phase 1 interviews conducted by UC Davis personnel, the interviewers were blind to study hypotheses and/or details of individual participants' prior experiences.

The caregivers of a few participants indicated that the adolescent or young adult had attempted to commit suicide in the past, had especially violent tendencies, or had cognitive difficulties and would likely not understand many of our questions. These individuals were sent a modified health and well-being survey that did not include any victimization or legal involvement questions. By avoiding the topics of victimization and legal involvement, the risk of exacerbating these individuals' problems—for example, by reminding them of traumatic or distressing experiences—was reduced. The modified surveys included demographic questions (e.g., regarding age, ethnicity, income, education) and health questions, which included the YASR, DES, Close Relationships Questionnaire, TSI, BSI, and SMAST. (These questionnaires overlapped with those administered to participants in other phases of the study.) Two participants completed these modified versions. Our results should be considered in light of the possibility that certain potential participants who were particularly distressed or violent either failed to enroll in the study or enrolled but completed only a subset of the measures.

Phase 2

Participants were mailed the Phase 2 measures and a letter asking them to complete the questionnaires. For the adolescents and young adults, the average length of time between Phase 1 and Phase 2 was 4.33 ($SD = .33$) months. Participants who failed to return the questionnaires were sent a duplicate set and/or were contacted by phone to complete the measures. One hundred and fourteen adolescents and young adults (87 targets and 27 controls) and 90 caregivers (65 targets and 25 controls) completed the Phase 2 questions by mail; 44 adolescents and young adults (36 targets and eight controls) and 46 caregivers (39 targets and seven controls) completed Phase 2 questionnaires over the phone; seven target adolescents and young adults and four target caregivers completed Phase 2 questionnaires during an in-person meeting. No significant differences on the mental health measures were evident between adolescents and young adults who completed Phase 2 via mail versus phone, t's (145–152) < 1.56.

III. CODING, ANALYTIC PLAN, AND PRELIMINARY ANALYSES

CODING

Coding schemes were developed to score participants' open-ended responses as well as other information collected in the project. For each item coded, at least two independent researchers scored no less than 12% of the data independently. Coders were blind to participants' specific abuse and legal experience history. Proportion of agreement was .80 or higher (range .80–1.00). Discrepancies were discussed and resolved, and the remaining data were scored by one or more of the raters.

Target Case Identification

Target adolescents' and young adults' responses were compared with the original CSA case documentation to determine whether they disclosed the target case (i.e., the case documented and studied in the 1992 project). Information that was compared included the name and/or identity of the perpetrator and the participant's relationship with the perpetrator. Additional information, compared when necessary, included the adolescent's or young adult's age when the abuse began and ended, the frequency and duration of the abuse, type of sexual activity, and the outcome of the legal case. Participants' responses during Phase 1 were classified as: (a) clear disclosure of the target case ($n = 142$), (b) no disclosure of the target case but clear disclosure of another CSA experience ($n = 7$), (c) disclosure of a CSA experience, but match to the target case was unverifiable ($n = 6$), or (d) no disclosure of CSA ($n = 19$), which included 17 who claimed never to have been sexually abused and 2 who reported knowing (e.g., from a parent) that they were sexually victimized, but having no memory of what happened (see Goodman et al., 2003, for details regarding predictors of disclosing CSA). Three individuals claimed that the original CSA allegations in the 1980s were false reports, but provided sufficient information to identify the target cases.

44

Socioeconomic Status (SES)

Data concerning caretaker occupation were collected at the time of the 1992 study. For the present purposes, this information was recoded using the 1989 Socioeconomic Index (Nakao & Treas, 1992, as printed in Entwisle & Astone, 1994). This SES index was based on 1980 census data concerning educational attainment and income of individuals in 503 detailed occupational categories. Codes range from 0 (low SES) to 100 (high SES). Reported occupations that were not precisely listed on the scale were matched with the occupation that they most closely resembled. Occupations that were insufficiently specific to be reasonably classified were considered missing. To create a single SES score for each participant, children with occupational information for only one parent were assigned that parent's score, whereas children with occupational information for more than one parent were assigned the higher SES score of the two parents.

Risk Index Scores

Consistent with a large number of studies concerning risk factors that contribute to developmental psychopathology (e.g., Masten & Wright, 1998; NICHD Early Child Care Research Network, 2004; Rutter, 1979; Werner & Smith, 1992), several risk scores were computed. Because a number of these risk factors could have stemmed from or been related to having experienced CSA in childhood, the risk scores were computed only for the legal involvement sample. Risk factors were defined as, "measurable characteristics of individuals that heighten the probability of a worse outcome in the future for groups of individuals who share the risk factor or who have more of the risk variables than a comparison group who does not have the risk factor or has less of the risk variable" (Masten & Wright, 1998, p. 10). Risk factors were identified by reviewing data collected during the 1992 study (e.g., SES, maternal mental health) and participants' open- and closed-ended responses during Phases 1 and 2 of the current study. Factors of interest were based on those described in research by Masten and Coatsworth (1998), Rutter (1979), and others (e.g., Sameroff et al., 1993; Williams et al., 1990) as conferring increased risk. Consistent with this research, risk factors were dichotomously identified as being present (1) or absent (0).

CSA Risk Index

Information from children's original CSA case files was coded (at the time of the 1992 study) for the severity of the sexual acts, the closeness of the relationship between the perpetrator and child, and the duration of the abuse. This information was used to create the CSA risk index. These three characteristics were selected based on the large body of research concerning

45

adverse effects of CSA which reveals that invasive physical assault, especially penetration, and experiencing intrafamilial abuse that occurs over long-time periods significantly increase the risk of adverse short- and long-term consequences (Berliner, 2004; Kendall-Tackett et al., 1993; Spaccarelli, 1994). The presence of each of these three characteristics, specifically, whether the abuse involved penetration, was perpetrated by a parent (biological or step), and lasted more than 1 day (i.e., involved repeated, longer lasting assault), was summed and divided by three to create the CSA risk index.

Family Risk Index

Factors that conferred increased risk in the family domain included: having been emotionally abused as a child by mother or father (each coded separately), not having been emotionally close in childhood to one's biological mother, having been physically neglected, witnessing parents engage in domestic violence, the mother or father having been jailed or having abandoned the child (all coded separately), parental divorce, being abused by a sibling, and having a parent who was addicted to drugs. Information on these experiences was gleaned from participants' Phase 1 responses. Two other factors were also included: low family SES at Time 1 (Time 1 corresponds to the start of the CSA legal case; scores of 30, unskilled laborer, or lower were classified as present on this risk factor) and maternal mental health problems at Time 1 according to the Social Adjustment Scale-Revised (scores above 2.25 on a scale ranging from 1 to 4, with higher scores indicating poorer adjustment, were classified as present for this risk factor; the cut-off corresponds to two standard deviations above the mean of a community sample reported in Weissman, 1978). The number of family risk factors present was summed and divided by the number of family risk factors available.

Trauma Risk Index

A trauma risk index score was calculated to reflect the number of adverse experiences, aside from ones captured in other risk variables and aside from the CSA, that the respondents had endured in childhood or adulthood, as reported in their Phase 1 responses. Experiences included: being the victim of a crime (including physical assault, burglary, child physical abuse, or any other crime, all coded separately), death of a loved one, lived in foster care or a group home, went in and out of foster homes, experienced a serious accident, failed out of school, had an unwanted pregnancy, experienced rape as an adult, and experienced domestic violence as an adult. Each separate occurrence of self-reported nontarget CSA experience was also counted. It was possible to confirm a number of these Phase 1 responses based on the 1992 study data. Because some participants were not yet 18 and hence could not have experienced adult rape, proportion trauma risk scores were calculated by summing the number of adverse experiences to which participants had been exposed and dividing by the number possible.

Legal Risk Index

Numerous characteristics of the legal case, as documented in the original 1992 study, were considered in a composite legal risk score. These included: the case being continued at least once, the case lasting more than 1 year (beginning with the report to authorities and ending with the close of the case), the child not receiving maternal support following the discovery of the abuse and/or during the legal case, the case lacking corroborative evidence, the child being involved in a concurrent dependency and neglect case, the child having testified in the case, and the defendant not serving a prison/jail sentence (e.g., case dismissed, probation). Again, proportion scores were calculated by summing present risk factors and dividing by the number of risk factors possible (i.e., 7).

ANALYTIC PLAN

The results are presented in three chapters. Briefly, in Chapter IV, we discuss the main findings concerning developmental and legal-experience predictors of long-term mental health outcomes. Outcomes of interest include trauma-related symptoms and general behavior problems. In Chapter V, we present results concerning developmental and legal-experience predictors of individuals' specific attitudes regarding the former legal case and general attitudes toward the legal system. Finally, in Chapter VI, we describe analyses concerning associations between participants' emotional reactions before testifying (i.e., their anxiety while waiting to testify) and later mental health problems and legal attitudes, and between participants' emotional reactions while testifying and later mental health problems and legal attitudes.

Our main hypotheses concerning predictors of mental health and attitudinal outcomes in the legal involvement sample were tested via hierarchical linear regression analyses. Whenever possible, other analytic procedures were also employed, for example, to examine changes over time in functioning and attitudes more precisely.[1] The regression analyses were designed to investigate the extent to which testifying was directly, as well as in conjunction with age and other CSA and legal characteristics, associated with long-term outcomes; and whether testifying remained an important predictor of long-term outcomes when other risk factors (e.g., family risk factors) that relate to adverse outcomes were considered concurrently.

In the regressions, all theorized predictors with the exception of the legal case characteristics were entered first to account for their associations with the outcomes prior to considering the legal case characteristics. These predictors included participants' age at Time 1, which corresponded to the start of the legal case; gender; CBCL T scores at Time 1; CSA risk index; family risk index; trauma risk index; and, when predicting legal attitudes, official arrest history. Two primary legal case characteristics, testify status and the severity of sentence in the legal case, were entered second. Testify status referred to a scaled variable with 1 = did not testify, 2 = testified once, and 3 = testified more than once. Sentence severity was also coded according to an ordinal scale, with 0 = case dropped/not guilty, 1 = deferred judgment, 2 = probation/no incarceration, 3 = county jail, and 4 = prison. Three hypothesized interactions were entered on the third step: (a) participants' age at Time 1 × testify status, (b) CSA risk index × testify status, and (c) sentence severity × testify status. Variables were entered into each regression analysis identically in three separate blocks, and all independent, continuous variables were centered before inclusion, according to guidelines proposed by Aiken and West (1991).

Although we focused our primary attention on testifying and case outcome as two main legal characteristics that might predict adverse consequences, we were also interested in the relations between other characteristics of participants' legal experiences and later psychological functioning and feelings toward the legal system. Additional analyses were thus conducted. These analyses concerned the number of times participants were interviewed about the CSA and participants' overall legal risk, that is, the total number of adverse events to which they had been exposed during their participation in the CSA legal case (see Chapters IV and V).

For individuals who went to court expecting to testify and individuals who actually did testify, documentation was available concerning their feelings about testifying and emotional reactions while testifying. Analyses concerning the associations between participants' emotional reactions and later mental health and attitudes are reported separately, in Chapter VI, because of the specific nature of the courthouse experiences and the smaller sample sizes available. (Only individuals who were at the courthouse waiting to testify reported on their anxiety, only individuals who testified had their emotional reactions rated while giving testimony.)

Finally, in Chapters IV and V, an additional set of analyses was conducted that compared long-term outcomes between the legal involvement and control groups. These analyses consisted primarily of 3 (age) × 3 (group status) analyses of covariance (ANCOVAs) and multivariate analyses of covariance (MANCOVAs). Participants' age was divided into three groups: 3–6, 7–11, and 12–17 years, based on their age at Time 1 (i.e., when the CBCL was complete), which corresponds to age when the legal case began for the legal involvement sample and a similar age for the control sample. These specific age categories were selected because first, developmental theories of coping with trauma indicate that the effects of life traumas, including maltreatment, vary depending on children's developmental level and on the salient developmental milestones of a given period. The preschool period, or 3–6 years, was distinguished from the middle school period because, at the earlier ages, children's relationships with caregivers and basic social skills are being developed, whereas at the later ages, peer relationships are a focal point of development. Children in the third age group, adolescence or ages 12–17 years, have more sophisticated cognitive abilities and may cope with negative life experiences, including legal involvement, differently than children in the younger groups. Second, in our study, we focused on participants' age at the time of the original legal case as opposed to their current age. The two ages are obviously highly correlated and thus could not be included in the same analyses. We were specifically interested in how the timing of exposure to legal involvement in childhood relates to later adverse outcomes, hence requiring that we focus on age at the start of the legal case. Group status refers to one of the three samples in the study design: victim/witnesses who testified in the former CSA case (i.e., *testifiers*), victim/witnesses who had not testified in the former CSA legal case (i.e., *nontestifiers*), and individuals who had no history of CSA or CSA-related legal involvement (i.e., *controls*). (Of note, group status here is different from testify status, which was described earlier. The latter refers to a scaled variable reflecting frequency of testifying and is included in analyses examining outcomes among only the legal involvement sample. Group status, as just described, concerns the entire study sample.)

In the ANCOVAs and MANCOVAs, participants' original CBCL *T* scores were covaried to take into account differences in mental health functioning prior to the start of the legal case. (Such control is imperative in determining how legal involvement per se, as opposed to pre-prosecution factors, affects long-term functioning). Also, gender was included as a factor in subsequent 2 (gender) × 3 (group status) analyses to test for differences between males' and females' long-term reactions to legal involvement.

Throughout the *Monograph*, all significant effects from analyses are reported. Effect sizes (e.g., partial η^2) are also provided. Finally, for ease in interpretation, nonadjusted means are presented when describing all results.

Preliminary analyses were conducted to identify differences in demographic characteristics by group status: Means across the three groups (testifiers, nontestifiers, and controls) for the primary demographic variables and covariates are presented in Table 5. No significant group differences were obtained when comparing the percentage of males or nonCaucasian participants, $\chi^2(2) < 5.17$. Nor did the three groups differ according to one-way ANOVAs predicting the delay between their age at Time 1 and their age when they completed the Phase 1 interview, or the delay between their completion of Phases 1 and 2 of the current study, F's ≤ 1.64.

One-way ANOVAs, did, however, reveal that the groups differed significantly in age at Time 1, family SES at Time 1 (which range from $0 =$ low to $100 =$ high), and original CBCL T scores (which range from 0 to 100, higher scores reflecting poorer adjustment), F's$(2, 190$ or $212) \geq 7.77$,

TABLE 5

SAMPLE CHARACTERISTICS BY GROUP STATUS (STANDARD DEVIATION)

	Group Status		
Sample Characteristic	Testifiers	Nontestifiers	Controls
Age in months at Time 1[a]	121.45 (45.88)	124.23 (41.62)	86.88 (28.45)
	$n = 53$	$n = 121$	$n = 41$
Gender (% female)	83	79	63
	$n = 53$	$n = 121$	$n = 41$
SES[b]	34.00 (18.43)	40.00 (19.32)	53.22 (26.26)
	$n = 43$	$n = 115$	$n = 25$
Ethnicity			
Caucasian (%)	52	68	64
Hispanic (%)	23	13	12
African American (%)	10	13	9
Other/multi-ethnic (%)	15	8	15
	$n = 52$	$n = 120$	$n = 33$
CBCL total T score at Time 1	64.89 (11.39)	61.60 (10.50)	57.24 (8.10)
	$n = 53$	$n = 121$	$n = 41$
Delay in years from Time 1 to	12.75 (.84)	12.67 (.90)	12.36 (1.72)
Phase 1 of current study	$n = 53$	$n = 121$	$n = 41$
Delay in months from Phase 1 to	3.94 (5.92)	5.02 (7.22)	3.09 (4.05)
Phase 2 of current study	$n = 42$	$n = 83$	$n = 32$
Official arrest record (%)[b]	35	38	6
	$n = 49$	$n = 121$	$n = 36$

Notes.—SES, socio-economic status, higher scores indicating higher income or SES; CBCL, Child Behavior Checklist, higher scores correspond to poorer adjustment.
[a]Time 1 corresponds to the start of the target CSA legal case for the legal involvement sample and, for all study participants, when the original CBCL was complete.
[b]Official arrest information was collected from local, state, and national databases.

p's < .01. At Time 1, the testifiers and nontestifiers were older and came from families with lower incomes than the control participants, F's(1, 90 or 212) $\geq$ 8.88, p's < .01. Testifiers and nontestifiers also had significantly higher CBCL T scores than the controls, F's(1, 212) $\geq$ 5.48, p's < .05. The testifiers and nontestifiers did not differ from each other in age, SES, and CBCL, F's(1, 212) $\leq$ 3.56, p's < .10. However, when the entire original 1992 sample was included rather than only participants from the original sample who completed the current study, the difference between the testifiers' and nontestifiers' initial CBCL scores became significant, $F(1, 214) = 5.37$, $p < .05$: testifiers had higher scores at the start of the case.

Finally, the two legal involvement groups were also more likely than the control group to have an official criminal arrest record, $\chi^2(2) = 12.11$, $p < .01$ (Table 5). Even though we attempted to match the control group to the legal involvement group by recruiting control participants partly from mental health clinics, it was still not possible to obtain individuals without a history of CSA who had comparable levels of CBCL-indexed behavior problems and arrest records. Finally, correlations revealed that participants' age at Time 1 was not significantly related to their gender, CBCL T scores, Time 1 SES, the delay between Time 1 and Phase 1 of the current study and between Phases 1 and 2 of the current study, or whether they had an official arrest record (r's ranged from $-.10$ to .13, df's ranged from 193 to 215).

Several additional sets of preliminary correlational analyses were conducted. The first concerned associations among the main dependent measures of interest in the study, that is, between the mental health and attitudinal outcomes. When the entire sample (legal involvement and control) was included, correlations between mental health and general legal attitudes (e.g., of the legal system's unfairness) painted a fairly consistent picture: Poorer adjustment (e.g., higher defensive avoidance, more internalizing symptoms) was associated with feeling that the legal system is more unfair, including to defendants; greater dissociative tendencies were associated with greater agreement that the legal system is too harsh on individuals accused of crimes (Table 6).

Second, correlations were computed between the target participants' current mental health functioning and attitudes toward the former target CSA legal case (Table 7). Because these correlations concerned attitudes toward the former CSA legal case, only legal involvement participants who disclosed the legal case in Phase 1 and answered the former case attitude questions (n's = 127 or 132) were included. Higher internalizing symptoms as indexed on the YABCL were associated with greater dissatisfaction with the outcome of the former CSA case.

Third, correlations were computed among the individual, proximal, and legal case predictors included in the regression analyses (see description

51

TABLE 6

BIVARIATE CORRELATIONS BETWEEN PARTICIPANTS' CURRENT MENTAL HEALTH SYMPTOMS
AND ATTITUDES TOWARD THE LEGAL SYSTEM, COMPUTED ON THE ENTIRE
(LEGAL INVOLVEMENT AND CONTROL) SAMPLE

| | General Legal Attitudes | | |
Mental Health Symptom	Unfairness of the Legal System[a]	System too Harsh on the Accused[b]	System too Harsh on Victims[b]
Trauma symptoms	$df = 168$	$df = 168$	$df = 168$
TSI sexual problems	− .02	− .12	− .01
TSI defensive avoidance	.17*	− .10	− .13
PTSD	.13	− .03	− .08
Dissociation	.05	− .22**	− .08
General mental health functioning	$df = 119–212$	$df = 116–209$	$df = 116–208$
YABCL internalizing	.19*	.05	− .05
YABCL externalizing	.13	.01	− .05
BSI	.14	− .11	− .08
YASR internalizing	.10	− .11	− .01
YASR externalizing	.20**	− .14	− .05

Notes.—TSI, Trauma Symptoms Inventory; PTSD, post-traumatic stress disorder (scored as a composite variable created from the TSI and Post-Traumatic Stress Diagnostic Scale symptoms subscales); YABCL, Young Adult Behavior Checklist; BSI, Brief Symptoms Inventory (scores reflects the average of the subset of the BSI items included in the interview); YASR, Young Adult Self-Report. All measures but the YABCL were completed by participants; the YABCL was completed by caregivers regarding participants. For all mental health measures, higher scores indicate poorer adjustment.
[a]Responses scored on a scale from 1 = very fair to 4 = very unfair.
[b]Responses scored on a scale from 1 = strongly agree to 4 = strongly disagree.
*$p < .05$.
**$p \leq .01$.

above concerning the regression models). These correlations, presented in Table 8, only included the legal involvement sample. When characteristics at the individual level (specifically, age, gender, and preprosecution mental health) were considered, being older at the start of the legal case was related to experiencing a greater number of life traumas in addition to the CSA and to having been interviewed more frequently in the original CSA legal case. However, being younger was associated with higher legal risk scores. Thus, even though the older participants had been questioned more, overall, the younger children were exposed to a greater number of adverse legal circumstances during their CSA case (e.g., continuances, lack of maternal support, testifying). Female victims experienced more invasive abuse than did male victims. Finally, higher preprosecution CBCL T scores were associated with experiencing a higher number of life traumas beyond those associated with CSA, having been arrested, and experiencing more adverse components during the CSA legal case. At the

TABLE 7

BIVARIATE CORRELATIONS BETWEEN TARGET PARTICIPANTS' CURRENT MENTAL HEALTH
SYMPTOMS AND ATTITUDES TOWARD THE FORMER TARGET CSA LEGAL CASE

| | Target Case Legal Attitudes | |
| | Effects of the | Dissatisfaction with |
Mental Health Symptom	Case on Life[a]	the Case Outcome[b]
Trauma symptoms	$df = 106$	$df = 106$
TSI sexual problems	$-.08$	.08
TSI defensive avoidance	.10	.11
PTSD	$-.01$	.02
Dissociation	.17	.00
General mental health functioning	$df = 70–132$	$df = 67–127$
YABCL internalizing	.09	.28*
YABCL externalizing	.07	.20
BSI mean	$-.04$	.07
YASR internalizing	$-.05$	.02
YASR externalizing	.05	.13

Notes.—Because the attitude questions being analyzed here concerned participants' feelings about the former target CSA legal case, only participants from the legal involvement sample who disclosed the target case were included in the correlations. TSI, Trauma Symptoms Inventory; PTSD, post-traumatic stress disorder (scored as a composite variable created from the TSI and Post-Traumatic Stress Diagnostic Scale symptoms subscales); YABCL, Young Adult Behavior Checklist; BSI, Brief Symptoms Inventory (scores reflect the average of the subset of the BSI items included in the interview); YASR, Young Adult Self-Report. All measures but the YABCL were completed by participants; the YABCL was completed by caregivers. For all mental health measures, higher scores indicate poorer adjustment.
[a]Responses scored on a scale from 1 = very positive to 4 = very negative.
[b]Responses scored on a scale from 1 = very satisfied to 4 = very unsatisfied.
*$p < .05$.

proximal level, adverse family events and life traumas beyond CSA were strongly associated with each other and to having a criminal arrest record. Finally, the legal risk index included testifying and the perpetrator receiving a lenient sentence, which explains the significant associations of legal risk to these characteristics.

Next, comparisons were made for the various risk and legal characteristics between individuals who had testified in their CSA case and individuals who had not testified. Means are presented in Table 9. No significant differences emerged between the two groups in the number of adverse family events (family risk index), CSA events (CSA index), or additional life stressors (trauma risk index) they had endured. Also, as described in the aforementioned group status analyses that also included the control participants, the testifiers and nontestifiers did not differ in age at Time 1, gender, SES, or delay from Time 1 to Phase 1 study participation. Again, however, original CBCL T scores differed when the entire sample was considered. Obviously, the two groups differed in the frequency with which

53

TABLE 8

BIVARIATE CORRELATIONS AMONG INDIVIDUAL, LEGAL, AND PROXIMAL PREDICTORS, COMPUTED ON THE LEGAL INVOLVEMENT SAMPLE

Predictor	1	2	3	4	5	6	7	8	9	10	11
N	174	174	174	173	174	174	170	169	171	81	171
1. Age at Time 1[a]	—										
2. Gender[b]	-.02	—									
3. CBCL total T at Time 1	.03	-.02	—								
4. Family risk index	.15	.14	.19*	—							
5. CSA risk index	.06	.18*	.09	.09	—						
6. Trauma risk index	.29**	.09	.27***	.52***	.05	—					
7. Official arrest record	.02	-.07	.23**	.19**	-.08	.26**	—				
8. Testify status[c]	-.02	.06	.10	.03	-.14	.06	-.02	—			
9. Sentence severity[d]	.02	-.03	.00	.07	.06	-.05	.11	-.14	—		
10. Number of interviews	.23*	.03	-.04	.03	.18	.02	.06	.07	.02	—	
11. Legal risk index[e]	-.18*	.01	.18*	.10	.04	.09	-.01	.68***	-.20*	-.01	—

Notes.—CBCL, Child Behavior Checklist (completed by caregivers); CSA, child sexual abuse.

[a]Time 1 corresponds to the start of the original target CSA legal case.

[b]Gender was coded as 1 = male, 2 = female.

[c]Testify status was scored according to an ordinal scale (1 = did not testify, 3 = testified more than once).

[d]Sentence severity was scored according to an ordinal scale (0 = acquitted/case dismissed, 4 = department of corrections/prison).

[e]The legal risk index included testifying and the perpetrator receiving a lenient sentence. For all risk indexes, higher scores reflect experiencing a greater proportion of adverse events.

*$p < .05$.

**$p \leq .01$.

***$p \leq .001$.

TABLE 9

MEAN RISK AND CASE CHARACTERISTIC SCORES BASED ON WHETHER PARTICIPANTS TESTIFIED OR NOT IN THE FORMER CSA LEGAL CASE

Risk and Legal Case Characteristic	Legal Involvement Group	
	Testifiers	Nontestifiers
	$n = 52–53$	$n = 116–121$
Family risk index	.30 (.18)	.27 (.19)
CSA risk index	.35 (.32)	.42 (.33)
Trauma risk index	.26 (.18)	.22 (.15)
Testify status[a]	2.32 (.52)	1.00 (.00)
Sentence severity[b]	2.54 (1.29)	2.40 (1.69)
Legal risk index	.47 (.13)	.21 (.15)

Notes.—[a]Testify status was scored according to an ordinal scale (1 = did not testify, 3 = testified more than once). [b]Sentence severity was scored according to an ordinal scale (0 = acquitted/case dismissed, 4 = department of corrections/prison); For all risk indexes, higher scores reflect experiencing a greater proportion of adverse events.

they had testified in the former case and in their legal risk scores (which included testifying as one of the risk factors). The groups did not differ in the severity of the perpetrator's sentence, however.

Although the aforementioned analyses concerned differences between the testifiers and nontestifiers overall, a final set of analyses concerned differences between former victim/witnesses who went to court expecting to testify (whether or not they actually did) and former victim/witnesses who never went to court expecting to testify. In particular, although 63 children in the 1992 study testified in their cases, 110 children went to the courthouse expecting to testify. Some of these cases resulted in a last-minute plea bargain, thereby eliminating the need for certain children to take the stand. In other cases, children did not testify for different reasons (e.g., a continuance delayed the hearing or trial). Because of the potential importance of the anxiety inherent in preparing to testify (as opposed to anxiety resulting from actually testifying), we examined how participants' emotional reactions while waiting related to their later mental health and attitudes. It was first important, however, to identify differences between individuals who waited at the courthouse expecting to testify and those who never went to the courthouse expecting to testify. Of participants who completed the current study, comparisons between those who went to the courthouse expecting to testify ($n = 82$) and those who never went to the courthouse (and hence never testified, $n = 78$) revealed several important differences, F's$(1, 158) \geq 6.37$, p's$<.01$: Participants who waited at court expecting to testify were older, $M = 135.04$, $SD = 39.93$, and had higher initial CBCL T scores, $M = 64.54$, $SD = 10.53$, than participants who had not waited at court; $M = 113.86$, $SD = 42.28$, and $M = 60.21$, $SD = 11.28$, for age in months and CBCL, respectively. Participants who waited at court also experienced less invasive abuse (i.e., had lower abuse risk index scores), $M = .34$, $SD = .32$, than participants who never went to court, $M = .48$, $SD = .34$. When the entire Goodman et al. (1992) sample is included, the results remain identical: individuals who went to court expecting to testify were older, had higher CBCL scores at the start of the legal case, and experienced less invasive abuse.

These patterns are important. Perhaps the older children were perceived by prosecutors as more able to testify, leading to their increased likelihood of going to court expecting to testify. Alternatively, defense attorneys may have questioned the older children's credibility or motives for alleging sexual abuse, reducing the defendant's willingness to plea. In either circumstance, older children's cases would be more likely to proceed to court, with children needing to be ready to testify. Disturbed children may not be perceived as credible or may be inconsistent during interviews, both of which could lead to lower likelihood of a plea bargain being accepted. In contrast, severe cases may have stronger corroborative evidence, leading to reduced likelihood of them ending up in court and the child needing to be ready to testify.

Insofar as our findings generalize nationally to CSA cases today, the fact that children who are already vulnerable, as indexed by their behavioral disturbance at the start of the case, are at increased likelihood of going to the courthouse expecting to testify may be a matter of some concern, given the stress inherent in expecting to testify. In any case, whether these children actually end up testifying is undoubtedly affected by myriad factors (e.g., whether the defendant accepts a plea bargain at the last minute, which occurs fairly frequently).

NOTE

1. In the present data set, other statistical techniques (e.g., structural equation models, hierarchical linear modeling) were not appropriate for several reasons. First, we were not tapping underlying, nonmeasurable constructs with our measures. Instead, most variables of interest consisted of simple and observable measures (e.g., relationship to the perpetrator, number of arrests). Second, it was not appropriate to infer temporal order among the different dependent measures (e.g., whether attitudes predicted global mental health functioning or vice versa), making it difficult to examine them in concurrent models. Third, the sample size limited us from identifying and investigating individual differences within subgroups. Thus, regression analyses were the most appropriate technique to test our study's main hypotheses.

IV. CURRENT MENTAL HEALTH

OVERVIEW

For many sexually victimized children, discovery of the abuse results in legal involvement. It is important to determine whether such involvement affects later mental health and whether the outcomes vary with development (the latter indexed as age at the start of the prosecution). Because of the extensive information available on our study participants (e.g., documentation of their legal experiences, a measure of behavioral adjustment at the start of the prosecution), we were able to examine these issues. We focused on predictors of participants' current levels of trauma-specific symptomatology as well as their more general psychological adjustment. Our analyses reveal how legal involvement and age at time of legal involvement relate to later psychological disturbance once emotional problems resulting from other traumatic experiences are taken into account.

MEASURES

Two sets of mental health measures were included. *Trauma-specific* measures included the subscales of the Trauma Symptom Inventory (TSI; completed by participants during Phase 2) that assessed sexual concerns, dysfunctional sexual behaviors, defensive avoidance, and post-traumatic stress symptomatology; the Dissociative Experiences Scale (DES), an index of dissociative tendencies; and the Post-Traumatic Diagnostic Scale (PDS), a measure of post-traumatic stress disorder (PTSD). The sexual concerns and dysfunctional sexual behavior subscales of the TSI identified similar kinds of symptoms and were strongly correlated, $r = .71$, $p < .001$. We therefore combined them into a single "sexual problems" scale. The PTSD subscale score from the TSI and the number of PTSD symptoms according to the PDS were also strongly correlated, $r = .59$, $p < .001$, and were thus combined (by averaging z-scores) into a single PTSD symptomatology score.

General mental health measures included the externalizing and internalizing subscales of the Young Adult Behavior Checklist (YABCL), which as mentioned earlier is an upward extension of the Child Behavior Checklist (CBCL), completed by caregivers in Phase 2; participants' mean responses on nine questions from the Brief Symptom Inventory (BSI) that were asked in Phase 1 (the items were moderately correlated, with r's ranging from .20 to .52, and formed a reliable composite with $\alpha = .81$); and the externalizing and internalizing symptom T scores from the Young Adult Self-Report (YASR), completed by participants in Phase 2. The YABCL and YASR scores were standardized according to age and gender norms (Achenbach, 1997; Achenbach & Rescorla, 2003).

For all mental health measures, higher scores indicate poorer adjustment or more severe symptoms. The means for age groups at Time 1 (4–6, 7–11, and 12–17 years) and group status (testifiers, nontestifiers, and controls) for the trauma-specific measures are presented in Table 10. Corresponding means for the general mental health symptom measures are presented in Table 11. Correlations among the measures are presented in Table 12. As can be seen in Table 12, participants' scores on the various measures were moderately to strongly correlated. Missing values were thus imputed using the expectation–maximization procedure to obtain maximum likelihood estimates (Little & Rubin, 1989). Only participants who completed at least one of the Phase 2 mental health measures were included when computing imputed values, and the number of individuals in the analyses with such values ranged from 14 for the DES to 16 for the TSI.

DO AGE AND TESTIFYING PREDICT MENTAL HEALTH OUTCOMES?

Our primary questions concerned whether children's age when they entered the legal case, along with the number of times they testified, predicts long-term mental health above and beyond mental health problems apparent at the start of the prosecution and other risk factors, such as those associated with the family context. Our hypotheses were as follows. First, consistent with former research indicating that early trauma onset is associated with negative long-term consequences, we expected that being younger at the time of the original case would be positively associated with later problems. We further expected these age differences in mental health outcomes to be particularly robust among individuals who testified multiple times (i.e., an age × testify status interaction), because the youngest children were least likely to understand the purpose of their legal participation and least likely to be able to cope emotionally with it (e.g., Compas, 1987; Davis et al., 2005; Saywitz et al., 1989). Second, based on results of the 1992 study, which revealed that testifying multiple times was associated with poor adjustment in the short-term, testifying repeatedly was hypothesized to continue to be associated with poor adjustment in the long term.

TABLE 10

MEANS FOR TRAUMA SYMPTOMS BY GROUP STATUS AND AGE AT TIME 1 (STANDARD DEVIATIONS)

	Group Status												
	Testifiers				Nontestifiers				Controls			
Trauma symptom	4–6 years	7–11 years	12–17 years	Mean	4–6 years	7–11 years	12–17 years	Mean	4–6 years	7–11 years	12–17 years	Mean
TSI sexual problems	5.14 (7.06) n = 12	5.38 (7.39) n = 12	5.97 (4.92) n = 21	5.59 (6.09) n = 45	3.31 (3.65) n = 16	4.21 (3.69) n = 27	3.79 (3.65) n = 47	3.83 (3.63) n = 90	3.29 (4.14) n = 16	3.69 (2.20) n = 13	4.40 (6.63) n = 5	3.60 (3.88) n = 34
TSI defensive avoidance	7.83 (7.22) n = 12	8.58 (7.96) n = 12	10.32 (4.81) n = 21	9.15 (6.37) n = 45	7.22 (6.44) n = 16	9.00 (4.89) n = 27	8.49 (5.44) n = 47	8.42 (5.44) n = 90	4.31 (4.03) n = 16	5.94 (4.81) n = 13	3.80 (3.35) n = 5	4.86 (4.23) n = 34
PTSD	.06 (1.11) n = 12	−.29 (.93) n = 12	.39 (.80) n = 21	.12 (.95) n = 45	−.13 (.96) n = 16	.04 (.86) n = 27	.13 (.91) n = 47	.06 (.90) n = 90	−.33 (.86) n = 16	−.17 (.60) n = 13	−.61 (.52) n = 5	−.31 (.72) n = 34
Dissociation	16.21 (15.22) n = 12	7.90 (8.03) n = 12	18.29 (14.04) n = 21	14.97 (13.53) n = 45	19.76 (12.67) n = 16	16.73 (15.22) n = 27	13.43 (13.07) n = 47	15.54 (13.75) n = 90	8.71 (10.52) n = 16	12.19 (9.33) n = 13	5.80 (4.26) n = 5	9.61 (9.46) n = 34

Note.—Measures were completed by adolescents and young adults during Phase 2. TSI, Trauma Symptoms Inventory, PTSD, post-traumatic stress disorder (scored as a composite variable created from the TSI and Post-Traumatic Stress Diagnostic Scale symptoms subscales). On all measures, higher scores indicate poorer adjustment.

TABLE 11

MEANS FOR GENERAL MENTAL HEALTH FUNCTIONING BY GROUP STATUS AND AGE AT TIME 1 (STANDARD DEVIATIONS)

General mental health functioning	Group status											
	Testifiers				Nontestifiers				Controls			
	4–6 years	7–11 years	12–17 years	Mean	4–6 years	7–11 years	12–17 years	Mean	4–6 years	7–11 years	12–17 years	Mean
YABCL internalizing	59.67 (10.08) n = 12	64.60 (9.07) n = 5	57.88 (10.02) n = 17	59.50 (9.89) n = 34	52.75 (6.22) n = 8	58.11 (7.48) n = 19	57.74 (9.68) n = 31	57.17 (8.66) n = 58	53.43 (11.07) n = 14	54.28 (5.53) n = 11	56.20 (7.63) n = 5	54.37 (8.64) n = 30
YABCL externalizing	65.58 (10.86) n = 12	62.80 (9.73) n = 5	55.29 (11.20) n = 17	59.32 (11.33) n = 34	56.75 (6.18) n = 8	57.26 (9.41) n = 19	55.29 (11.62) n = 31	56.13 (10.23) n = 58	55.00 (6.53) n = 14	51.55 (7.94) n = 11	53.60 (4.77) n = 5	53.50 (6.82) n = 30
BSI mean	2.29 (.85) n = 16	2.16 (.76) n = 12	2.28 (.84) n = 24	2.25 (.81) n = 52	2.01 (.74) n = 22	2.12 (.78) n = 37	2.10 (.70) n = 61	2.09 (.71) n = 120	1.94 (.61) n = 19	1.88 (.56) n = 15	1.90 (.55) n = 7	1.91 (.57) n = 41
YASR internalizing	53.527 (15.33) n = 12	50.33 (12.82) n = 12	55.01 (11.64) n = 22	53.40 (12.83) n = 46	49.35 (14.04) n = 17	51.73 (10.45) n = 27	54.24 (11.18) n = 47	52.58 (11.58) n = 91	50.44 (13.10) n = 16	49.33 (8.68) n = 13	50.40 (6.99) n = 5	50.01 (10.58) n = 34
YASR externalizing	55.28 (13.66) n = 12	49.42 (15.41) n = 12	55.85 (10.63) n = 22	54.02 (12.81) n = 46	53.24 (14.15) n = 17	54.14 (10.55) n = 27	53.74 (7.99) n = 47	53.76 (10.02) n = 91	52.57 (10.44) n = 16	51.48 (8.39) n = 13	48.80 (7.98) n = 5	51.63 (9.19) n = 34

Note.—The YABCLs were completed by caregivers during Phase 2; the BSI was completed by adolescents and young adults during Phase 1 (scores reflect the average of the subset of the BSI items included in the interview); the YASR was completed by adolescents and young adults during Phase 2. YABCL, Young Adult Behavior Checklist; BSI, Brief Symptoms Inventory; YASR, Young Adult Self-Report. On all measures, higher scores indicate poorer adjustment.

TABLE 12

BIVARIATE CORRELATIONS AMONG THE MENTAL HEALTH MEASURES IN THE ENTIRE
(LEGAL INVOLVEMENT AND CONTROL) SAMPLE

Mental health measure	1	2	3	4	5	6	7	8
df	87–149	88–105	93–151	89–151	94–122	94–120	160	161
1. TSI sexual problems	—							
2. TSI defensive avoidance	.49***	—						
3. PTSD	.48***	.72***	—					
4. Dissociation	.48***	.40***	.46***	—				
5. YABCL internalizing	.24*	.25*	.35*	.30**	—			
6. YABCL externalizing	.20*	.21*	.17^t	.28**	.69***	—		
7. BSI mean	.27**	.43***	.44***	.35***	.48***	.42***	—	
8. YASR internalizing	.51***	.33**	.45***	.40***	.38***	.33***	.40***	—
9. YASR externalizing	.53***	.53***	.65***	.38***	.46***	.18***	.53***	.65***

Notes.—TSI, Trauma Symptoms Inventory; PTSD, post-traumatic stress disorder (scored as a composite variable created from the TSI and Post-Traumatic Stress Diagnostic Scale symptoms subscales); YABCL, Young Adult Behavior Checklist; BSI, Brief Symptoms Inventory (scores reflects the average of the subset of the BSI items included in the interview); YASR, Young Adult Self-Report. All measures but the YABCL were completed by participants; the YABCL was completed by caregivers regarding participants. For all measures, higher scores indicate poorer adjustment.
$^t p < .10.$
$^* p < .05.$
$^{**} p \leq .01.$
$^{***} p \leq .001.$

Third, two additional interactions involving having testified were hypothesized: a testify status × CSA risk interaction and a testify status × sentence severity interaction. Regardless of any post-abuse experiences, enduring severe abuse (e.g., penetration) perpetrated by a family member should be associated with poorer later adjustment. However, a testify status × CSA risk interaction was hypothesized because the adverse effects of enduring incest are likely to be exacerbated when children repeatedly recount in open court what happened. In contrast, not testifying about less severe abuse might also lead to increased problems, partly because participants might have wanted to have their day in court. The testify status × sentence interaction was expected because mental health problems might also arise for individuals who did not testify and then the perpetrator was deemed not guilty or received a lenient sentence. In such cases, participants might feel they could have done more to achieve justice.

Our hypotheses were tested with a series of regression analyses predicting trauma-specific symptomatology and general mental health. In these regressions, variables unrelated to the legal case were entered first, as described in Chapter III. These included children's age at the start of the legal case (i.e., age at Time 1), gender, CBCL total T score, trauma risk index, family risk index, and CSA risk index (i.e., invasiveness of participants' CSA experience). On the second step, two legal case characteristics—frequency of testifying (i.e., testify status) and sentence severity—were entered. These case characteristics, as distinct from the composite legal risk index score, were considered based on prior research suggesting the salience of both testifying and case outcome as predictors of subsequent mental health (e.g., Goodman et al., 1992; Sas, 1993). Additional analyses, to be described later, focused on participants' general legal risk scores. On the third step of the regressions, three interaction terms were entered: testify status $\times$ age at Time 1, testify status $\times$ CSA risk index, and testify status $\times$ sentence severity. All variables were centered prior to their inclusion. Bivariate correlations between the predictors and the mental health outcome measures are shown in Table 13.

Trauma-Specific Symptoms

We focused first on trauma-specific behavior problems, which, according to prior research (Briere et al., 1995), are often more strongly associated with former CSA than are global mental health symptoms. The trauma-specific measures concerned sexual problems, defensive avoidance, dissociation, and PTSD. For sexual problems, the model was significant, $F(11, 117) = 1.91$, $p < .05$, and explained 15% of the variance. Significant predictors, listed in Table 14, included the number of times participants testified and the testify status $\times$ CSA risk index interaction. Testifying a greater number of times was associated with increased sexual problems. A plot of the interaction (see Figure 1) revealed that, among individuals who experienced invasive abuse, testifying repeatedly was associated with higher levels of self-reported sexual problems, whereas not testifying was associated with fewer problems. In contrast, among individuals who experienced less invasive abuse, frequency of testifying was unrelated to sexual problems. Stated another way, as is evident in the figure and consistent with our hypothesis, the highest number of self-reported sexual problems was reported by individuals who testified multiple times about particularly invasive abuse.

The model predicting participants' defensive avoidance symptoms was also significant, $F(11, 117) = 2.07$, $p < .05$, overall $R^2 = .16$ (Table 14). The only significant finding was a testify status $\times$ CSA risk index interaction. A plot of the interaction (Figure 2) revealed that, among individuals who testified multiple times, a trend indicated increasing defensive avoidance symptoms as the invasiveness of the abuse increased. This is similar to the pattern for sexual problems. However, the highest levels of defensive avoidance were evident among individuals who had not testified when the

TABLE 13

BIVARIATE CORRELATIONS BETWEEN INDIVIDUAL, LEGAL, AND PROXIMAL PREDICTORS AND MENTAL HEALTH MEASURES IN THE LEGAL INVOLVEMENT SAMPLE

	Trauma Symptoms				General Mental Health Functioning				
Predictors	TSI Sexual Problems	TSI Defensive Avoidance	PTSD	Dissociation	YABCL Internalizing	YABCL Externalizing	BSI Mean	YASR Internalizing	YASR Externalizing
df	132–136	131–135	131–135	131–135	90–92	90–92	169–172	133–137	133–137
Age at Time 1[a]	.07	.10	.19*	−.10	.01	−.21*	.01	.13	.03
Gender[b]	−.02	.06	.05	−.11	.03	.13	−.02	−.10	−.10
CBCL total T at Time 1	.12	.18*	.09	.14	.44***	.43***	.28***	.18*	.10
Family risk index	.09	.20*	.21*	.03	.32**	.23**	.18*	.12	.08
CSA risk index	.03	−.05	.05	−.05	.12	.01	.02	.01	−.02
Trauma risk index	.14	.23**	.27**	.04	.25**	.31**	.27***	.23**	.18*
Testify status[c]	.18*	.01	−.01	−.06	.13	.10	.09	−.01	.04
Sentence severity[d]	−.04	−.04	−.08	−.04	.02	−.02	.07	−.06	−.04

Notes.—TSI, Trauma Symptoms Inventory; PTSD, post-traumatic stress disorder (scored as a composite variable created from the TSI and Post Traumatic Stress Diagnostic Scale symptoms subscales); YABCL, Young Adult Behavior Checklist; BSI, Brief Symptoms Inventory (scores reflects the average of the subset of the BSI items included in the interview); YASR, Young Adult Self-Report. All measures but the YABCL were completed by participants; the YABCL was completed by caregivers regarding participants. For all measures, higher scores indicate poorer adjustment.

[a]Time 1 corresponds to the start of the original target CSA legal case.

[b]Gender was coded as 1 = male, 2 = female.

[c]Testify status was coded according to an ordinal scale (1 = did not testify, 3 = testified more than once).

[d]Sentence severity was scored according to an ordinal scale (0 = acquitted/case dismissed, 4 = department of corrections/prison).

*$p < .05$.

**$p \leq .01$.

***$p \leq .001$.

TABLE 14

LINEAR REGRESSION RESULTS DEPICTING THE COMBINED PREDICTORS OF CURRENT MENTAL HEALTH IN THE LEGAL INVOLVEMENT SAMPLE

Predictor	Mental Health Symptoms			
	TSI Sexual Problems	TSI Defensive Avoidance	YABCL Internalizing	YABCL Externalizing
	Standardized β			
Step 1				
Age at Time 1[a]	.04	.04	− .01	− .26**
Gender[b]	.02	.10	.01	.13
CBCL total T at Time 1	.10	.14	.41***	.38***
Family risk index	.03	.10	.29*	.15
CSA risk index	.01	− .11	− .01	− .06
Trauma risk index	− .02	.07	.06	.30**
Step 2				
Testify status[c]	.23*	− .02	.24*	.18[t]
Sentence severity[d]	.05	.04	.00	.00
Step 3				
Age × testify	− .01	.11	− .14	− .06
CSA risk × testify	.30***	.19*	.18[t]	.07
Sentence × testify	− .13	− .19[t]	.25**	.25**

Notes.—For TSI sexual problems: $F(11, 117) = 1.91, p < .05$, overall $R^2 = .15$; the R^2 at step 1 = .03, n.s., the $R^2\Delta$ at Step 2 = .03, n.s., and the $R^2\Delta$ at step 3 = .09, $p < .01$. For TSI defensive avoidance: $F(11, 117) = 2.07$, $p < .05$, overall $R^2 = .16$; the R^2 at step 1 = .08, $p < .10$, the $R^2\Delta$ at step 2 = .00, n.s., and the $R^2\Delta$ at Step 3, = .08, $p < .05$. For YABCL internalizing: $F(11, 75) = 4.43, p < .001$, overall $R^2 = .29$; the R^2 at step 1 = .28, $p < .001$, the $R^2\Delta$ at step 2 = .02, n.s., and the $R^2\Delta$ at step 3 = .10, $p < .05$. For YABCL externalizing, $F(11, 75) = 4.89$, $p < .001, R^2 = .42$; the R^2 at step 1 = .35, $p < .001, R^2\Delta$ at step 2 = .01, n.s., and $R^2\Delta$ at step 3 = .06, $p < .10$. TSI, Trauma Symptoms Inventory, completed by participants; YABCL, Young Adult Behavior Checklist, completed by caregivers. For all measures, higher scores indicate poorer adjustment.
[a]Time 1 corresponds to the start of the original target CSA legal case.
[b]Gender was coded as 1 = male, 2 = female.
[c]Testify status was coded according to an ordinal scale (1 = did not testify, 3 = testified more than once).
[d]Sentence severity was scored according to an ordinal scale (0 = acquitted/case dismissed, 4 = department of corrections/prison).
[t]$p < .10$.
*$p \leq .05$.
**$p \leq .01$.

abuse was less invasive. In line with our hypothesis, individuals who did not testify about minimally invasive abuse may have felt that their claims were not believed or that, because they did not testify, their allegations were not taken seriously, leading to increased efforts to avoid thinking about the negative events. The regression models predicting dissociation and PTSD symptoms were not significant.

Overall, these findings suggest that testifying a greater number of times is associated later with increased sexual problems and defensive avoidance,

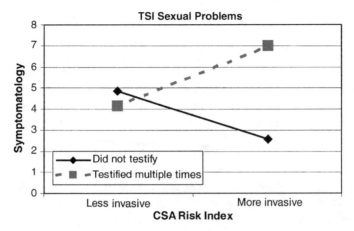

FIGURE 1.—Frequency of sexual problems reported on the Trauma Symptoms Inventory (TSI) as a function of the invasiveness of participants' CSA experience (CSA risk index) and testify status. Higher scores reflect greater symptomatology, and the end points on the plot denote one standard deviation above and below the means for each predictor.

especially when CSA is intrafamilial and more severe (e.g., involving penetration). In addition, the results indicate that not testifying is associated with greater defensive avoidance if the CSA is extrafamilial and less severe (e.g., nongenital fondling). While refraining from causal inference, it is of interest that testifying multiple times—the strongest mental health predictor in the short term—also predicted trauma-related mental health nearly a decade after the children entered the criminal justice system.

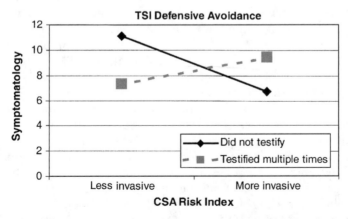

FIGURE 2.—Frequency of defensive avoidance symptoms on the Trauma Symptoms Inventory (TSI) as a function of the invasiveness of participants' CSA experience (CSA risk index) and testify status. Higher scores reflect greater symptomatology, and the end points on the plot denote one standard deviation above and below the means for each predictor.

Given that we uncovered some important associations between prior legal experiences and trauma-specific symptoms among former CSA victims, it was also important to determine the extent to which similar associations emerged when the victims' general mental health was considered.

The study participants' former caretakers (typically their mothers) completed the YABCL, which provides measures of internalizing and externalizing problems. Participants' YABCL internalizing T scores were regressed on the predictor variables (the predictors were identical to those described in the preceding analyses). The model was significant, $F(11, 75) = 4.43, p < .001$, and explained 39% of the variance. Participants' CBCL T scores at the start of the original legal case, their family risk index score, the number of times they testified, and the testify status × sentence severity interaction were significant (Table 14). Having a higher CBCL score at the start of the legal case was associated with higher current levels of internalizing problems, as was having been exposed to a greater number of risk factors in one's family environment. Supporting our predictions and replicating the results of our original study (Goodman et al., 1992), testifying more frequently was associated with internalizing problems.

The significant interaction revealed, however, that this pattern was moderated by the outcome of the case. As can be seen in Figure 3, heightened levels of internalizing symptoms were evident among individuals who testified repeatedly when the perpetrator received a heavy sentence. Perhaps these individuals felt particularly upset about the extent of their legal involvement (i.e., testifying repeatedly) and felt their efforts were still not vindicated despite a relatively tough sentence for the perpetrator. Indeed, as will be evident later, these individuals also held more negative attitudes toward the legal system and toward individuals accused of crime.

Next, participants' YABCL externalizing behavior problems were examined. The overall model was again significant, $F(11, 75) = 4.89, p < .001$, and explained 42% of the variance. At the final step, participants' age when the original legal case began, their trauma risk factor score, their original CBCL T score, and the testify status × sentence severity interaction were significant (Table 14). Consistent with our hypotheses, having been younger when the legal case began was associated with higher levels of externalizing behavior problems. Although one might speculate that individuals who were younger at the time of the original case were also younger at follow-up, and certain types of externalizing symptoms (e.g., aggression, acting out, delinquency, drug/alcohol use) peak in late adolescence and early adulthood (e.g., Moffitt, 1993), the YABCL is standardized for age. Thus, age-normative differences in such behavior are taken into account in the scores. Instead, these results reveal, as hypothesized, that being younger

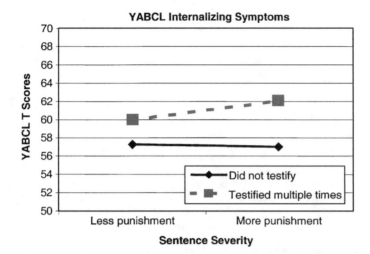

FIGURE 3.—Young Adult Behavior Checklist (YABCL) internalizing *T* scores as a function of sentence severity and testify status. Higher scores reflect greater symptomatology, and the end points on the plot denote one standard deviation above and below the means for each predictor.

rather than older as a victim in a CSA criminal case may be more deleterious in terms of later functioning, specifically, in acting-out behavior problems.

With regard to participants' trauma risk index and former CBCL scores, both were positively associated with externalizing problems. Finally, the significant testify status × sentence severity interaction (see Figure 4) was similar to that observed for internalizing symptoms. The highest levels of externalizing symptoms were evident among individuals who testified multiple times against a perpetrator who was severely punished, and the lowest levels were evident among individuals who did not testify against a perpetrator who was severely punished.

Finally, the three self-reported general mental health measures were entered into separate regressions. For participants' BSI mean, the model was significant at step 1, $F(6, 157) = 4.21$, $p < .001$, $R^2 = .14$ (the $R^2\Delta$ was nonsignificant at steps 2 and 3). Only participants' CBCL total T score emerged as a significant predictor, $\beta = .21$, $p < .01$: Higher CBCL T scores at the time of the original study were associated with poorer self-reported adjustment years later. The model predicting participants' internalizing behaviors on the YASR was significant at step 1, $F(6, 123) = 2.31$, $p < .05$, $R^2 = .10$. Participants' trauma risk index emerged as a significant predictor, such that experiencing a greater proportion of adverse life experiences, in addition to the CSA and other familial risks, was associated with higher levels of internalizing symptoms, $\beta = .21$, $p = .05$. Finally, the model predicting externalizing behaviors on the YASR was not significant.

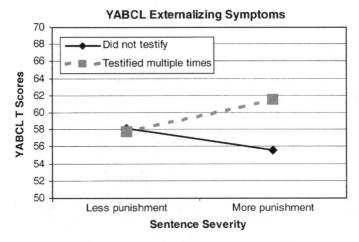

FIGURE 4.—Young Adult Behavior Checklist (YABCL) externalizing *T* scores as a function of sentence severity and testify status. Higher scores reflect greater symptomatology, and the end points on the plot denote one standard deviation above and below the means for each predictor.

Changes in Mental Health Over Time

In the 1992 study, behavioral disturbance decreased for most of the children who were followed from the start of the prosecution through the later assessments (e.g., after having testified). However, a subset of children showed no improvement or greater behavioral disturbance in the short term. Improvement was defined as a CBCL *T* score at the final follow-up, in the late 1980s, that was lower than the CBCL *T* score at the start of the legal case (i.e., Time 1). Lack of improvement was defined as a CBCL *T* score equal to or higher at the 1980s follow-up than the start of the case. Significant predictors of lack of improvement included testifying multiple times, not receiving maternal support, and not having corroborative evidence confirming the abuse (Goodman et al., 1992).

If there are long-term adverse effects of testifying, one would expect that children identified as nonimprovers in the 1992 study would continue to be less well adjusted over time than children identified as improvers. In addition, insofar as legal involvement at a young age is associated with greater behavior problems later, as suggested by our analyses predicting externalizing symptoms, age at entry into the prosecution might similarly predict the maintenance of poor functioning over time. To test these possibilities, we examined whether participants' prior status as improvers or nonimprovers predicted their current YABCL internalizing and externalizing *T* scores. We were especially interested in the YABCL because the improvement classifications in the 1992 study were based on the

68

caregiver-completed CBCL, and the YABCL, which was also completed by caregivers in the present study, is an upward extension of the CBCL. In a series of regressions, we first entered participants' age at Time 1, CBCL total T scores at Time 1, original improvement status (i.e., improver vs. nonimprover at Time 1), and the number of times they testified (on the three-point testify status scale: never, once, more than once). We then entered the improve × testify status interaction to test the prediction that testifiers who had not improved initially would continue to exhibit relatively poor functioning. Because of the small number of participants eligible for these analyses (i.e., only individuals who were followed throughout the original study had data concerning their initial improvement), relatively few predictors could be included.

When participants' YABCL externalizing scores were entered, the model was significant, $F(5, 23) = 2.75$, $p < .05$, and explained 37% of the variance (step 1 $R^2 = .20$, n.s.; step 2 $R^2\Delta = .17$, $p < .05$). At step 2, as already reported in the regression analyses conducted on the entire sample, higher original CBCL T scores were positively associated with current externalizing symptoms, $\beta = .40$, $p < .05$. Additionally, the interaction between whether participants had improved in the original study and the number of times they testified was significant, $\beta = -.43$, $p < .05$. When plotted, the significant interaction (Figure 5) revealed that, among individuals who had not improved initially, whether they testified or not was unrelated to later externalizing symptoms. Among individuals who had improved initially, testifying multiple times was now associated with increased externalizing problems. In fact, only the improvers who had not testified in the target CSA case appeared to be functioning relatively well at the time of the present study, at least in terms of having lower externalizing symptoms than those of the other participants. When participants' YABCL internalizing scores were entered as the dependent measure, the model was not significant, $F(5, 23) = 1.45$.

In the 1992 study, both maternal support and corroborative evidence emerged as significant predictors of improvement among the testifiers. As mentioned, because of the limited sample size in these analyses, it was not possible to enter other variables concurrently into regressions predicting the older adolescents' and adults' current functioning among improvers and nonimprovers. Thus, analyses were reconducted including the following as additional predictors in separate regressions: (a) maternal (or nonoffending caregiver) support following the discovery of the abuse and during the legal case, and (b) corroborative evidence, each coded dichotomously as present or absent. These variables were entered on step 2, with the same variables described above (participants' age at the start of the legal case, original CBCL, improver status, and testify status) entered on step 1 and the improver × testify status interaction entered on step 3. The inclusion of maternal support significantly increased the amount of variance

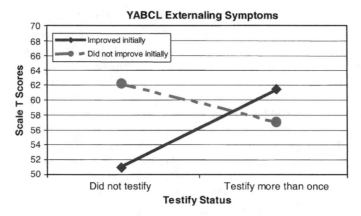

YABCL Externaling Symptoms

FIGURE 5.—Young Adult Behavior Checklist (YABCL) externalizing T scores as a function of whether participants improved in the short term following participation in the legal case and testify status. Higher scores reflect greater symptomatology, and the end points on the plot denote one standard deviation above and below the means for each predictor.

in internalizing symptoms accounted for, step 2 $R^2\Delta = .16$, $p < .05$; overall model $F(5, 22) = 2.70$, $p < .05$, overall $R^2 = .38$. Not receiving maternal support following the discovery of the CSA predicted higher internalizing scores over a decade later, $\beta = -.41$. The inclusion of corroborative evidence did not significantly increase the explanatory power of the models.

Legal Risk and Number of Interviews

Although we focused mainly on testifying in court and age as combined predictors of long-term outcomes, findings from several studies suggest that other features of child victim/witnesses' legal experiences also affect their later functioning (e.g., Sas, 1993). Additionally, consistent with studies highlighting the importance of indexing cumulative and domains of risk (e.g., Deater-Deckard et al., 1998; NICHD Early Child Care Research Network, 2004), adverse outcomes may be less a function of exposure to one particular adverse experience and more a function of multiple, additive risks. The availability of extensive information from the original legal case enabled us to test associations between other components of participants' CSA legal experiences and their later mental health. First, we examined participants' legal risk index score (described in Chapter III) as a predictor of their current mental health. These scores reflected the number of adverse aspects of the legal case to which participants had been exposed (e.g., lack of corroborative evidence, taking part in a concurrent dependency case, having testified). Second, we examined associations between the number of interviews participants had endured during the target legal case and their later trauma symptomatology and general mental health. Data concerning number of interviews were collected at the end of the 1992 study from the subset of caretakers ($n = 89$) who had taken part in the final phase of the original study. Of these, 81 participants completed the current study. No significant differences emerged in the number of times caregivers reported that their child had been interviewed based on whether participants completed the current study or not, $t(87) = -.01$. Among individuals in the current study, the mean number of interviews was 5.01, $SD = 4.25$, range $= 0–25$. The smaller number of individuals for whom interview data were available precluded us from including this variable in the legal risk score or adding it as an additional predictor in the regressions analyses. Thus, interview number was analyzed separately.

In our preliminary analyses (Chapter III), correlations revealed that being younger when one's legal case began was associated with exposure to more legal risks during the time of the CSA prosecution. Insofar as participants who were younger at the time of the legal case were exposed to more adverse events during their legal involvement and had higher levels of externalizing symptoms, it is of interest to determine whether the younger participants' legal risk scores account for the evident associations between age and externalizing symptoms reported earlier.

To examine associations between legal risk and current mental health, we correlated participants' legal risk scores and their trauma-related symptoms and general mental health scores. Age at the start of the legal case and CBCL total T scores were controlled statistically because they could affect the legal case itself (e.g., whether the case was continued) and participants' later mental health. No significant relations were uncovered, r's ranged from $-.04$ to $.12$. Thus, the number of legal risk factors to which the child had been exposed did not explain current functioning better than did the number of times the child testified (as described earlier in the regression analyses). Nor did legal risk mediate the associations between age and externalizing symptoms reported previously. Instead, young age at the time of legal involvement and repeatedly testifying emerged as independent, important predictors of later functioning, the latter in conjunction with participants' CSA risk and the severity of the perpetrator sentence.

Second, we examined later mental health in relation to the number of interviews participants had endured during their childhood legal case. There were two significant associations between number of interviews and current mental health indicators (age at the start of the legal case and original CBCL scores were controlled—age because it was significantly associated with number of interviews and CBCL scores because of their significant association with current mental health). Experiencing more interviews was associated with higher self-reported dissociative tendencies, $r(64) = .27$, $p < .05$, and internalizing symptoms, $r(63) = .25$, $p < .05$. Thus, consistent with previous research, number of interviews seems to be an important source of stress for children in CSA investigations, stress that, in this case, may increase subsequent risk for mental health problems.[2]

Summary

Through our analyses, we identified several important predictors of mental health for the legal involvement sample. First, although the developmental trends were not robust across the different mental health measures, as predicted, being younger at the time of the original legal case was associated with more severe externalizing symptoms. Moreover, although participants who were younger tended to have also endured numerous adverse experiences during their legal case, their current behavior problems were not simply a function of their greater exposure to such experiences. Instead, having to endure legal involvement as a result of their sexual abuse experiences may have been especially difficult for younger individuals, leading to poorer mental health over time.

Second, when legal case characteristics were considered, testifying repeatedly was associated with poorer later mental health, including more trauma-related symptoms and more severe internalizing and externalizing behavior problems. The associations between testifying and poorer functioning remained even for individuals who had improved in the short term. Moreover, the total number of legal risk factors experienced was not significantly related to participants' current mental health. Accordingly, testifying in the adversarial system appears to be a salient feature in and of itself with direct implications for negative outcomes, including years after legal cases have ended.

Several additional findings highlight the importance of considering participants' CSA experiences and the outcome of their cases when evaluating long-term sequelae of testifying in court. Testifying frequently about particularly severe abuse—that is, abuse characterized by more risk characteristics—was associated with higher levels of later trauma-related problems. This appears to provide evidence for long-term adverse consequences of publicly and repeatedly recounting severe CSA, an experience that may reinforce individuals' self-perceptions as victims. The experience may also contribute later to oversexualized behaviors. Yet, when the abuse was less invasive or when the cases ended in a not guilty or lenient sentence, not testifying was associated with greater problems. Feeling that they could have done more to affect the outcome of the case may have led participants in our study who had not testified to experience greater frustration, anxiety, and concerns about not being believed, all of which might cause them later to avoid thinking about negative events or to evince other behavior problems. Finally, although some participants were faring better than the others, it is important to note that the participants' mental health was generally not very good.

HOW DID THE LEGAL INVOLVEMENT SAMPLE'S MENTAL HEALTH COMPARE WITH THAT OF THE NONABUSED CONTROL GROUP?

We also developed several hypotheses concerning differences in current functioning between individuals with versus without a history of CSA and CSA-related legal involvement. We specifically predicted that the former victim/witnesses, especially those who were younger when their case began and who testified at a younger age, would exhibit poorer adjustment later on than individuals with no CSA-related experiences, even when initial behavior problems were controlled statistically. We also predicted a gender by legal involvement interaction such that females in the two legal involvement groups would exhibit higher levels of internalizing problems (e.g., anxiety problems), and males in the two legal involvement groups would exhibit higher levels of externalizing symptoms. These effects were expected to be particularly pronounced among former victims who had testified. These hypotheses were tested with 3 (age) × 3 (group status: testifiers, nontestifiers, and control participants) ANCOVAs and MANCOVAs, followed by 2 (gender) × 3 (group status) analyses, as described next. In all analyses, participants' CBCL T scores were covaried to control for differences across groups in preprosecution mental health (see Table 5), differences that may have resulted from the CSA itself. SES also differed across the three groups, but missing data for a few of the oldest control participants precluded us from covarying SES in the full 3 (age) × 3 (group status) analyses. All results were confirmed in follow-up one-way ANCOVAs and MANCOVAs that included SES as an additional covariate.

Trauma-Specific Symptoms

We entered the sexual problems and defensive avoidance scores, both of which were derived from the TSI to tap trauma symptoms and thus were considered concurrently, into a MANCOVA. The main effect of group status was significant, $F(4, 316) = 3.03$, $p < .05$, $\eta^2 = .04$. Univariate analyses detected a significant effect for defensive avoidance, $F(2, 159) = 3.61$, $p < .05$, $\eta^2 = .04$. Planned comparisons revealed that both individuals who had testified and individuals who had not testified in the former legal case reported higher levels of defensive avoidant symptoms than individuals with no CSA or legal involvement history, F's $(1, 159) \geq 10.24$, p's $< .01$. The difference between testifiers and nontestifiers was not significant (see Table 10).

Next, participants' PTSD composite score and DES score were entered as dependent measures into separate 3 (age) × 3 (group status) ANCOVAs (Table 10). There were no significant main effects or interactions.

Thus, in regard to trauma symptoms, the main difference between the legal involvement samples and the control group was in defensive avoidance. The study participants who had histories of CSA and legal involvement reported greater tendencies than did the control individuals to avoid reminders of their past.

General Mental Health

We next examined age and legal involvement as combined predictors of participants' general mental health (age × group status means are presented in Table 11). Measures included the YABCL, completed by caregivers about participants, and the BSI items and YASR, completed by participants.

The YABCL and YASR have clinically derived cut-off levels, which correspond to scores at or above 64, and borderline clinical ranges, which correspond to scores between 60 and 63. A simple examination of participants' scores revealed that greater percentages of the legal involvement groups routinely fell in the borderline or clinical range than did the controls. For instance, among the 122 participants whose caregivers completed the YABCL, 42% of the legal involvement participants (47% of the testifiers and 40% of the nontestifiers) and 33% of the control participants fell in the marginal or clinical range for internalizing symptoms; 41% of the legal involvement sample (47% of the testifiers and 38% of the nontestifiers) and 20% of the control sample fell in the borderline or clinical range for externalizing symptoms. For participants' self-reported YASR scores, 33% and 26% of the testifiers and nontestifiers fell into the marginal or clinical range for externalizing symptoms, whereas 18% of the controls did. Finally, for internalizing symptoms, 33% of the testifiers, 23% of the nontestifiers, and 18% of the controls had scores in the borderline or clinical range. To determine whether aforementioned percentages differed statistically as a function of legal involvement and/or testifying, logistic regressions were conducted predicting whether participants' scores were at or above the borderline clinical range. Group status (testifiers, nontestifiers, controls) was entered categorically (dichotomously coded) along with participants' age in months at Time 1 and CBCL T scores. Group status was not significant in any of the logistic regressions.

Because it was more informative to treat the mental health scores as continuous measures rather than as dichotomous scores, the latter of which simply reflected whether or not individuals' scores were above or below the clinical cut-off point, we next examined more precisely whether participants' general level of mental health problems varied as a function of their age and group status, controlling for their preprosecution mental health. First, the two caregiver-completed YABCL scores (internalizing and externalizing) were entered into a 3 (age) × 3 (group status) MANCOVA (these dependent measures were entered concurrently because they were strongly related, see Table 11, and because both were tapping problem behaviors). Participants' CBCL total T scores were covaried. Although the multivariate effect of age was significant, $F(4, 222) = 2.75, p < .05, \eta^2 = .05$, neither of the univariate age effects was significant (Table 11).

Second, the three self-report measures (BSI mean, and YASR internalizing and externalizing scores) were examined. When participants' BSI means were entered into a 3 (age) × 3 (group status) ANCOVA, no significant main effects or interactions emerged. Nor did any significant effects emerge in a 3 (age) × 3 (group status) MANCOVA with YASR internalizing and externalizing symptoms entered.

Overall, then, in terms of general mental health, we failed to detect significant differences between the legal involvement and control samples (but see gender analyses). It should be kept in mind, however, that the individuals in the control group were selected from the start to have high levels of childhood behavioral problems. Thus, the lack of difference in general mental health is not surprising.

Gender

To test our predictions regarding interactions between gender and group status, we reconducted the aforementioned trauma-specific and general mental health ANCOVAs and MANCOVAs substituting gender for age, the latter of which was then entered as a covariate (as a continuous variable) along with participants' original CBCL T score at the start of the legal case. None of the main effects of gender nor the gender × group status interactions were significant. However, when DES was entered into the 2 (gender) × 3 (group status) ANCOVA, the group status main effect was significant, $F(2, 161) = 3.52, p < .05, \eta^2 = .04$. As is evident in Table 10, testifiers' and nontestifiers' DES mean scores were higher than were the control participants' scores, planned comparison F's$(1, 161) > 4.29, p$'s $< .05$. The difference between the testifiers and nontestifiers was nonsignificant. Thus, individuals in the legal involvement samples reported greater dissociative tendencies than did individuals in the control group.

Summary

Analyses comparing the three age and three legal involvement groups (testifiers, nontestifiers, and controls) revealed differences in trauma-related functioning based on group status, as expected. Individuals who testified and individuals who had not testified, that is, both groups of individuals who had experienced CSA and legal involvement, reported a greater number of defensive avoidance and dissociative symptoms than did individuals with no such history. These differences are all the more remarkable when one considers that the individuals in the control sample were selected

75

to have high levels of childhood behavioral problems. The differences likely reflect continuing adverse consequences of childhood sexual abuse or other adverse life experiences, as well as CSA-related legal involvement, for individuals in the legal involvement sample compared with individuals with no prior history of either CSA or CSA-related legal involvement.

We hypothesized that participants' age would interact with their group status to predict differences in mental health functioning such that individuals who testified when they were especially young would evidence the highest levels of mental health problems later. These patterns were not found. Finally, our predictions concerning gender × group status interactions were not supported.

The lack of robust developmental differences in mental health functioning across the three groups does not imply that CSA-related legal involvement was without consequences. Instead, our analyses reveal that, once individuals' mental health functioning at the outset of the legal case was controlled statistically, testifying in the CSA legal case did not increase participants' mental health symptoms compared with the symptoms exhibited by a matched control group of individuals, the latter of whom also showed considerable mental health problems in childhood. However, these analyses did not focus on how the associations between specific aspects of individuals' legal experiences and mental health outcomes varied developmentally. These analyses also did not include control for various risk factors in the children's lives. As seen from our earlier analyses involving the CSA victim/witnesses only, when statistically controlling for the individuals' domains of risk, earlier age at entry into the criminal justice system and having testified repeatedly were significant predictors of current mental health functioning.

NOTE

2. Although we did not collect data on the quality of therapy or the person's level or type of symptoms before entering therapy (precluding causal statements about the effects of therapy on later functioning), at the end of the Phase 1 interview, participants were asked if they had ever been in therapy or seen a counselor, therapist, or psychologist. All but two participants answered this question. Among the testifiers, 86% answered yes; among the nontestifiers (i.e., individuals involved in CSA cases who did not testify), 77% answered yes; among the controls (i.e., individuals with no known CSA or CSA-related legal experiences), 58% answered yes. The group status effect was significant, $\chi^2 = 9.12$, $p < .01$. Also, although there were no significant interactions between age group (3–6, 7–11, 12–17) × group status predicting whether individuals had been in therapy, a significant age effect emerged: A significantly smaller percentage of the youngest participants (58%) reported having been in therapy than the two older groups of participants, 7–11 = 79% and 12–17 = 83%, $\chi^2 = 12.81$, $p < .01$. In bivariate correlations with age partialled, a number of significant associations emerged between whether participants attended therapy and their current mental health problems. In all cases, having attended therapy was positively associated with symptomato-

logy, r's ranged from .21 to .28 for having been in therapy and the following: sexual problems, defensive avoidance, PTSD symptoms, YABCL internalizing symptoms, and YASR internalizing symptoms. When therapy attendance was included in the mental health analyses as an additional predictor, the variable was not significant in any of the models reported in the text, and its inclusion did not affect any of the results. The model predicting PTSD symptoms became significant, however, with attending therapy being the only significant predictor of PTSD symptoms. Given that we did not collect information on the quality of therapy or the duration of participants' involvement in therapy, we are hesitant to try to interpret these correlations in relation to long-term outcomes following CSA-related legal involvement.

V. ATTITUDES TOWARD THE LEGAL SYSTEM

OVERVIEW

Childhood legal involvement, in addition to its apparent influence on mental health, may also have a more subtle influence. Namely, involvement as a victim/witness in a CSA prosecution may also affect later attitudes toward the legal system, perceptions of justice, and feelings about the fairness of one's former legal experiences. Our study examined this possibility. We investigated whether the age at which victim/witnesses took part in the legal case was related to their later attitudes about the legal system. In the 1992 study, older victim/witnesses (e.g., individuals who were adolescents at the time of the prosecution) and females felt the most negatively about the legal system's fairness. Of particular interest here is whether these patterns are sustained over time and whether age and gender interact with testifying to influence later legal attitudes.

MEASURES

In Phase 1 of the current study, questions were included about participants' attitudes toward the legal system generally and toward the target case specifically. One set of questions concerned the CSA victim/witnesses' perceptions of their specific case. Participants rated the effects of the legal case on their life (1 = very positive to 4 = very negative) and their dissatisfaction with the case outcome (1 = very satisfied to 4 = very unsatisfied). Participants who reported having testified in the target case rated the effects of testifying on their life (1 = very positive to 4 = very negative), whereas participants who reported not having testified in the target case rated the effects of not testifying on their life (1 = very positive to 4 = very negative). We sought to identify significant predictors of their answers to these questions. Moreover, because several of the questions were identical to those asked of participants in the 1992 study, we could investigate changes in attitudes over time.

78

To assess general legal attitudes, we first asked participants to rate the fairness of criminal courts, police practices, and juvenile courts on a four-point scale (very fair to very unfair). A mean "unfairness" score was created, with higher scores reflecting greater perceived unfairness. The items were combined to assess general perceptions of the legal system rather than attitudes about individual components of the system and to reduce the risk of Type I errors.

Second, we asked participants to rate their level of agreement/disagreement with the following two statements: "The U.S. criminal courts are too harsh on people accused of crimes" and "The U.S. criminal courts are too harsh on victims of crime" (responses ranged from 1 = strongly agree to 4 = strongly disagree). Thus, for the question regarding defendants, higher scores indicate proprosecution/victim attitudes; for the question regarding victims, higher scores indicate prodefense attitudes.

Finally, in Phase 2, participants rated separate questions concerning the fairness of the legal system to children who allege physical abuse, sexual abuse, or exposure to domestic violence; and to parents who allege their children experienced physical abuse, sexual abuse, or domestic violence exposure. Analyses of the legal involvement participants' responses to these questions failed to reveal any significant predictors. Nor did any significant differences emerge between the legal involvement and control groups. Thus, these questions are not considered further.

Means for the attitude ratings by age and group status are presented in Table 15. Correlations among the ratings are presented in Table 16.

DO AGE AND TESTIFYING PREDICT ATTITUDES REGARDING THE FORMER CSA CASE?

An important goal of our study was to determine how the former victim/ witnesses felt about their prior legal experiences, including whether their feelings varied based on their age when the CSA case occurred, whether they testified, and the outcome of the case. Because we focused specifically on participants' attitudes toward the target CSA legal case, those who either failed to disclose the documented CSA or refused to talk about it (and hence were not asked questions about their feelings toward the CSA legal case, $n = 33$) were excluded (see Goodman et al., 2003, for details concerning participants' disclosure of the former CSA).

We hypothesized that being older at the start of the legal case and experiencing invasive abuse, especially in conjunction with later having to testify repeatedly, would be associated with more negative feelings about the target case. The perpetrator receiving a lenient sentence was further

TABLE 15

MEANS FOR THE ATTITUDE MEASURES BY GROUP STATUS AND AGE AT TIME 1 (STANDARD DEVIATIONS)

	Group status											
	Testifiers				Nontestifiers				Controls			
Legal Attitude	4–6 years	7–11 years	12–17 years	Mean	4–6 years	7–11 years	12–17 years	Mean	4–6 years	7–11 years	12–17 years	Mean
Target case												
Effects of the case on life[a]	2.23 (1.09) $n=13$	2.91 (1.22) $n=11$	2.76 (1.34) $n=21$	2.64 (1.25) $n=45$	2.00 (1.05) $n=10$	2.55 (1.27) $n=29$	2.75 (1.16) $n=48$	2.60 (1.20) $n=87$	—	—	—	—
Dissatisfaction with the case outcome[b]	2.20 (1.03) $n=10$	2.73 (1.01) $n=11$	2.48 (1.17) $n=21$	2.48 (1.18) $n=42$	2.20 (1.03) $n=10$	2.21 (.92) $n=28$	2.55 (.97) $n=47$	2.40 (.97) $n=85$	—	—	—	—
General												
Unfairness of the legal system[c]	2.25 (.57) $n=16$	2.19 (.58) $n=9$	2.44 (.77) $n=22$	2.33 (.67) $n=47$	2.52 (.46) $n=22$	2.45 (.56) $n=37$	2.46 (.46) $n=61$	2.47 (.49) $n=120$	2.31 (.39) $n=15$	2.38 (.55) $n=15$	1.94 (.55) $n=6$	2.28 (.45) $n=36$
System too harsh on the accused[d]	3.00 (.97) $n=16$	2.33 (.87) $n=9$	2.91 (.97) $n=22$	2.83 (.96) $n=47$	2.64 (.90) $n=22$	2.64 (.93) $n=36$	2.95 (.87) $n=61$	2.80 (.90) $n=119$	2.83 (.80) $n=12$	3.00 (.78) $n=14$	3.17 (.41) $n=6$	3.00 (.72) $n=35$
System too harsh on victims[d]	2.81 (.91) $n=16$	2.11 (1.05) $n=9$	2.27 (.88) $n=22$	2.43 (.95) $n=47$	2.65 (.75) $n=20$	2.53 (1.06) $n=36$	2.33 (1.04) $n=61$	2.44 (1.00) $n=117$	2.47 (.83) $n=15$	2.47 (.83) $n=15$	2.67 (.82) $n=6$	2.50 (.81) $n=36$

Notes.—Because the target case legal attitude questions concerned participants' feelings specifically about the former target CSA legal case, only target participants who disclosed the case in Phase 1 were included.

[a]Responses scored on a scale from 1 = very positive to 4 = very negative.

[b]Responses scored on a scale from 1 = very satisfied to 4 = very unsatisfied.

[c]Responses scored on a scale from 1 = very fair to 4 = very unfair.

[d]Responses scored on a scale from 1 = strongly agree to 4 = strongly disagree.

TABLE 16

BIVARIATE CORRELATIONS AMONG THE LEGAL ATTITUDE MEASURES

Legal Attitude	1	2	3	4
1. Effects of the case on life[a]	—			
2. Dissatisfaction with the case outcome[b]	.66***	—		
3. Unfairness of the legal system[c]	.41**	.35**	—	
4. System too harsh on the accused[d]	−.06	−.09	−.10	—
5. System too harsh on victims[d]	−.21*	−.10	−.16*	.02

Notes.—For correlations including the target case legal attitude questions (items 1 and 2), only legal involvement sample participants who disclosed the target case in Phase 1 were included, df ranged from 124 to 132. For correlations within the general legal attitude questions (items 3–5), the entire (legal involvement and control) sample was included, df ranged from 206 to 209.
[a]Responses scored on a scale from 1 = very positive to 4 = very negative.
[b]Responses scored on a scale from 1 = very satisfied to 4 = very unsatisfied.
[c]Responses scored on a scale from 1 = very fair to 4 = very unfair.
[d]Responses scored on a scale from 1 = strongly agree to 4 = strongly disagree.
*$p < .05$.
**$p < .01$.
***$p < .001$.

hypothesized to be associated with more negative attitudes toward the case. This was expected to be particularly likely when the lenient sentence was combined with not having testified in the case.

Predictors of Victims' Attitudes Toward the Former Case

We first investigated whether participant age and testifying, in conjunction with other potentially important individual and family factors, as well as CSA factors and other life stressors, predicted participants' ratings of the effect of the former legal case on their lives ($n = 127$) and their dissatisfaction with the outcome of the case ($n = 132$). Each measure was entered separately into a regression analysis. Predictors were virtually identical to those in the regressions predicting mental health, with one exception: Participants' official criminal record history (described in Chapter III) was included as an additional predictor because contact with the legal system as a defendant could affect current attitudes (Indermaur, 1994; Tyler, 1984). Predictors unrelated to the legal case were entered first and included participant age at Time 1, gender, CBCL T scores, trauma risk index, family risk index, CSA risk index, and criminal record. Second, the two key case characteristics (the number of times participants testified and sentence severity) were entered. Third, the three interaction terms were entered: testify status × age at Time 1, testify status × CSA risk index, and testify status × sentence severity (step 3). Correlations between the predictors and participants' case-specific attitudes are presented in Table 17.

The model predicting participants' ratings of the effects of the case on their lives was significant, $F(9, 106) = 3.39, p < .01$, and explained 22% of the

81

TABLE 17

BIVARIATE CORRELATIONS BETWEEN THE PREDICTORS AND ATTITUDE MEASURES IN THE LEGAL INVOLVEMENT SAMPLE

| Predictor | Target Case Legal Attitudes | | General Legal Attitudes | | |
	Effects of the Case on Life[a]	Dissatisfaction With the Case Outcome[b]	Unfairness of the Legal System[c]	System too Harsh on the Accused[d]	System too Harsh on Victims[d]
df	122–127	127–132	166–171	166–169	164–167
Age at Time 1[e]	.12	.16	.00	.14	−.17*
Gender[f]	.11	.30***	−.01	−.08	−.10
CBCL T at Time 1	.06	.09	.13	−.05	.01
Family Risk Index	.18*	.07	.09	−.05	−.04
CSA Risk Index	.13	.13	−.00	.04	.01
Trauma Risk Index	.27**	.22**	.22**	.01	−.21**
Official criminal record	.20*	.15	.22**	−.22**	.02
Testify status[g]	.07	.04	−.14	−.04	−.06
Sentence severity[h]	−.27	−.34***	−.06	.05	.18*

Notes.—For correlations concerning participants' target case legal attitudes, only legal involvement sample participants who disclosed the target case in Phase 1 were included; for correlations concerning participants' general legal attitudes, the entire legal involvement sample was included. CBCL, Child Behavior Checklist; CSA, child sexual abuse.

[a]Responses scored on a scale from 1 = very positive to 4 = very negative.
[b]Responses scored on a scale from 1 = very satisfied to 4 = very unsatisfied.
[c]Responses scored on a scale from 1 = very fair to 4 = very unfair.
[d]Responses scored on a scale from 1 = strongly agree to 4 = strongly disagree.
[e]Time 1 corresponds to the start of the original target CSA legal case.
[f]Gender was coded as 1 = male, 2 = female.
[g]Testify status was scored according to an ordinal scale (1 = did not testify, 3 = testified more than once).
[h]Sentence severity was scored according to an ordinal scale (0 = acquitted/case dismissed, 4 = department of corrections/prison).

*p < .05.
**$p \leq$ .01.
***$p \leq$ .001.

variance. Significant predictors included CSA risk, having a criminal record, and the severity of the perpetrator's sentence. Having endured more invasive abuse (e.g., abuse that involved penetration and/or was committed by a parent) and having been arrested for committing a crime predicted more negative feelings about the effects of the case on participants' lives. The perpetrator receiving a lenient sentence was similarly associated with more negative feelings (see Table 18).

TABLE 18

LINEAR REGRESSION RESULTS DEPICTING PREDICTORS OF PARTICIPANTS' ATTITUDES ABOUT
THE FORMER CASE AMONG PARTICIPANTS WHO DISCLOSED THE TARGET CASE IN PHASE 1

	Target Case Attitudes	
	Effects of the Case on Life[a]	Dissatisfaction with the Case Outcome[b]
Predictor	Standardized Betas	
Step 1		
Age at Time 1[c]	.04	.14
Gender[d]	.02	.25*
CBCL total T at Time 1	− .02	.02
Family risk index	.05	− .07
CSA risk index	.18*	.13
Trauma risk index	.12	.06
Official arrest record	.20*	.20*
Step 2		
Testify status[e]	.03	− .01
Sentence severity[f]	− .33***	− .33***
Step 3		
Age × testify	—	—
CSA risk × testify	—	—
Sentence × testify	—	—

Note.—For the model predicting participants' ratings of the effect of target case on their life, step 2 $F(9, 106) = 3.39$, $p < .01$, the overall R^2 at step 2 = .22; R^2 at step 1 = .11, $p < .10$, $R^2\Delta$ at step 2 = .11, $p < .01$, and $R^2\Delta$ at step 3 = .02, n.s. For the model predicting participants' dissatisfaction with target case outcome, $F(9, 111) = 5.07$, $p < .001$, the overall R^2 at step 2 = .29; R^2 at step 1 = .19, $p < .01$, $R^2\Delta$ at step 2 = .10, $p < .01$, and $R^2\Delta$ at step 3 = .03, n.s. CBCL, Child Behavior Checklist; CSA, child sexual abuse.
[a]Responses scored on a scale from 1 = very positive to 4 = very negative.
[b]Responses scored on a scale from 1 = very satisfied to 4 = very unsatisfied.
[c]Time 1 corresponds to the start of the original target CSA legal case.
[d]Gender was coded as 1 = male, 2 = female.
[e]Testify status was scored according to an ordinal scale (1 = did not testify, 3 = testified more than once).
[f]Sentence severity was scored according to an ordinal scale (0 = acquitted/case dismissed, 4 = department of corrections/prison).
*$p < .05$.
***$p < .001$.

Somewhat different predictors emerged when participants' dissatisfaction with the case outcome was examined. The model was again significant, $F(9, 111) = 5.07$, $p < .001$, and explained 29% of the variance. At step 2, consistent with the regression predicting participants' ratings of the effects of the legal case on their lives, having been arrested and lenient perpetrator sentences were both associated with greater dissatisfaction with the outcome of the CSA case (Table 18). Gender was also a significant predictor, with females, $M = 2.80$, $SD = 1.16$, being, on average, somewhat dissatisfied with the case outcome, and males, $M = 1.89$, $SD = 1.15$, being, on average, slightly positive about the outcome of the case, a pattern that is similar to the one observed in the 1992 study.

Together, these findings suggest that, even 14 years (on average) after involvement in a CSA legal case, females continued to hold negative attitudes, as did individuals who experienced severe abuse, and, most noteworthy, individuals whose case resulted in no or minimal perpetrator punishment. Finally, having had contact with the legal system not only as a victim, but also as a defendant, was related to feeling greater negativity about the system's response in the CSA case.

Effects of Testifying and Not Testifying on Victims

Next, we examined participants' ratings of the effects of testifying or not testifying. We first conducted a one-way age (age at Time 1: 4–6, 7–11, 12–17 years) ANOVA with participants' ratings of the effects of testifying in the target case as the dependent measure. The sample size in the analysis, $n = 37$, was small because only participants who actually testified and answered the Phase 1 questions about the effects of testifying were included. No significant age effects were obtained. Participants' mean rating of effect of testifying was 2.73, $SD = .96$.

We could not conduct a similar one-way (age at Time 1) ANOVA predicting participants' ratings of the effects of not testifying because too few of the youngest participants answered this question during the Phase 1 interview. The question asked whether there was a time when they "wanted to testify but did not get to or did not want to testify and did not have to." Participants who assented were asked to describe the experience and rate the effects of not testifying. Twenty-five participants assented and described the target CSA legal case. The correlation between age at Time 1 and feelings about having not testified was $r(25) = .35$, $p < .05$ (one-tailed), indicating that individuals who were older at the time of the CSA case were later more negative about not having testified. The mean of participants' ratings about the effects of not testifying was 2.56, $SD = 1.26$. This mean did not significantly differ from the mean rating of the effects of testifying made by participants who reported having testified in the case.

Next, the effects of perpetrator sentence (no jail/prison vs. jail/prison; the variable redefined here because of the small sample size) on participants' feelings about having testified or not were examined in one-way ANCOVAs, age at Time 1 covaried. The effect of sentence was significant when participants' ratings of the effects of testifying was included, $F(1, 34) = 4.26$, $p < .05$, $\eta^2 = .11$. Participants rated the effects of testifying more negatively when the perpetrator did not spend time in jail or prison, $M = 3.14$, $n = 14$, compared with when he did, $M = 2.48$, $n = 23$. A similar significant effect of sentence was obtained when nontestifiers' ratings were examined in a separate ANCOVA, $F(1, 20) = 4.95$, $p < .05$, $\eta^2 = .20$. Participants rated the effects of not testifying more negatively when the perpetrator was not jailed, $M = 3.00$, $n = 15$, compared with when he was jailed, $M = 2.13$, $n = 8$. Thus, whether participants testified in the target case or not, their perceptions of this experience were more negative when the perpetrator was not overtly punished.

Changes in Victims' Attitudes Over Time

As already mentioned, at the end of the 1992 study, participants who had been followed throughout their case were asked to rate the effects of the legal case on their life (response options ranged from very positive to very negative) and their dissatisfaction with the case outcome (response options ranged from very satisfied to very unsatisfied). Because identical questions were asked in this (the current) follow-up study, we were able to assess how these attitudes changed over time. The sample size in these analyses was reduced to 45 because of the smaller number of participants in the 1992 study who had answered these questions. Relevant to the representativeness of the sample included in these analyses, the proportion of testifiers is significantly larger than the comparable proportion from the 1992 study, $\chi^2(1) = 8.20$, $p < .01$. The over-representativeness of the testifiers in the present sample resulted in large part because the testifiers were the primary individuals (along with the matched group of nontestifiers) targeted for follow-up in the short-term study. Hence, the testifiers were disproportionately likely, at the end of their participation in the original study, to have been asked the aforementioned attitude questions about the CSA case. No other significant differences (i.e., in gender, criminal record, trauma risk index, family risk index, abuse risk index, or original CBCL total T scores) emerged between individuals included and not included, however.

Two 3 (age) × 2 (time period: end of the original study vs. Phase 1 of current study) mixed factorial ANOVAs were conducted, with participants' attitude ratings at each time entered as dependent measures. For participants' ratings of the effects of the legal case on their lives, a significant age × time interaction, $F(2, 42) = 5.26$, $p < .01$, $\eta^2 = .20$, was obtained (see Table 19). Simple effects analyses and planned comparisons revealed that participants who were particularly young, that is, between 4 and 6 years of age, at the time of the original study became significantly less negative in their ratings. In other words, their mean ratings of the effects of the legal case on their lives shortly after the case ended were significantly higher (corresponding to perceptions of more negative effects) than their later ratings and than the ratings of all other groups at both time periods, F's$(1, 42) \geq 3.25, p$'s $\leq .05$ (Table 19). In contrast, for individuals in the two older age groups at the end of their cases, their initial and later perceptions of the effects of the legal case on their lives did not differ significantly. When participants' satisfaction with the target case outcome was examined, neither the main effect of age or time nor their interaction was significant.

When a dichotomous testified variable (testified vs. not testified; the variable dichotomized because of the small sample size) was substituted for age in two similar ANCOVAs (with age at Time 1 covaried), no significant effects of testifying emerged. Thus, participants' ratings of the effects of the case on their lives and their satisfaction with the outcome did not vary as a function of whether they testified in their case. Their current feelings about the effects of the case on their lives and satisfaction with the case outcome both fell, on average, in the neutral to mildly negative range (Table 19).

Legal Risk and Number of Interviews

A final set of analyses concerned whether participants' legal risk index scores and the number of interviews in which the individuals took part as children predicted their current attitudes about the target case. Correlations, with participants' age at Time 1, CBCL T scores, and official arrest record partialled, failed to reveal any significant associations. Thus, neither the cumulative legal risk score nor the number of times the victim/witnesses were interviewed was related to their current attitudes about the effects of the CSA case on their lives, their present satisfaction with the legal case outcome, or their feelings about having testified or not.

Summary

Several of our predictions concerning case-specific attitudes were confirmed. Over time, participants' negative feelings about the effects of the legal case on their life dissipated somewhat, especially among individuals who were particularly young when the target case began. Gender was related to participants' current attitudes regarding their former case, with females reporting less satisfaction with the case outcome than males. Females experienced more invasive abuse than males, which may have led to their greater dissatisfaction with the case outcome that resulted. However, CSA risk was also considered in the regression analyses and did not relate to

TABLE 19

PARTICIPANTS' ATTITUDES ABOUT THE TARGET CASE AT THE END OF THE 1992 STUDY AND IN PHASE 1 OF THE PRESENT STUDY

	Time							
	End of 1992 Study[a]				Phase 1 of Current Study			
Target case attitude	4–6 years	7–9 years	10–17 years	Mean	4–6 years	7–9 years	10–17 years	Mean
Effects of target case on life[b]	3.67	2.20	2.76	2.88	2.00	2.70	2.41	2.37
N	6	10	29	45	6	10	29	45
Dissatisfaction with target case outcome[c]	2.5	2.75	1.93	2.39	2.17	3.36	2.37	2.64
N	6	8	27	41	6	8	27	41

Notes.—Only participants who completed the Goodman et al. (1992) follow-up and disclosed the target case in Phase 1 were included.
[a]Participants who were followed throughout their legal cases in the Goodman et al. (1992) study answered these questions shortly after their legal cases had ended.
[b]Responses at both times were scored on a scale ranging from 1 = very positive to 4 = very negative.
[c]Responses at both times were scored on a scale ranging from 1 = very satisfied and 4 = very unsatisfied.

participants' satisfaction, suggesting that other differences—for instance, in attributions regarding CSA and CSA-related legal involvement—contributed to the evident gender differences in satisfaction with the case outcome. Sentence severity did not differ between female and male victims (see Table 8, for correlation coefficients). In partial support of our hypothesis concerning age, among individuals who reported having not testified in the CSA case, being older was associated with more negative feelings about not having testified. Older children are more cognizant of the legal system's function and the implications of their involvement, which may have led to their more negative feelings about not having had their day in court. Finally, consistent with our hypotheses and with findings from the original study, the outcome of the target case continued to be strongly related to participants' current case-specific attitudes, with individuals whose perpetrator was acquitted or received a lenient sentence (e.g., probation) continuing to feel particularly negative about effects of the legal case on their lives and to be dissatisfied with the case outcome. Moreover, these associations held whether participants testified in their case or not.

DO AGE AND TESTIFYING PREDICT GENERAL ATTITUDES REGARDING THE LEGAL SYSTEM?

We next investigated how legal case characteristics relate to general perceptions of the legal system in the CSA former victim/witnesses. These analyses, without the nonabused controls, permit us to include variables specific to the CSA legal cases when examining predictors of long-term attitudes.

Fairness and Victim/Defendant Treatment Ratings

We hypothesized that the victim/witness being older at the time of the target case and the perpetrator receiving a less severe sentence would be associated with more negative feelings about the legal system. We also hypothesized that testifying would interact with the invasiveness of the abuse and the outcome of the case in predicting later attitudes. Testifying repeatedly in a case involving invasive abuse was expected to be associated with more negative attitudes. However, not testifying in a case involving minimally or noninvasive abuse was expected to be associated with feelings that the system is not harsh enough on defendants, especially if the defendant in the child's own case received a light sentence or the case was dismissed. These predictions were tested via regression analyses, with predictors being identical to those described previously in the case-specific attitude analyses. Predictors included children's age at the start of the legal case, gender,

CBCL total T score, trauma risk index, family risk index, CSA risk index, and official arrest record (step 1); testify status and sentence severity (step 2); and the testify status $\times$ age, testify status $\times$ CSA risk index, and testify status $\times$ sentence severity interactions (step 3). Correlations between the predictors and attitude measures are presented in Table 17.

For mean fairness ratings ($n = 171$), there were no significant effects at any step. The model predicting participants' disagreement with the statement, "The courts are too harsh on people accused of crimes" ($n = 169$), was significant, $F(12, 145) = 2.10, p < .05, R^2 = .15$. As is evident in Table 20, significant predictors included participants' age when the legal case began, whether they had been arrested for a crime, and the testify status $\times$ sentence interaction. As expected, being older when the CSA case began was associated with stronger disagreement that the courts are too harsh on individuals accused of crimes. Also, and not surprisingly, having been arrested was associated with greater agreement with the statement. The interaction, plotted in Figure 6, revealed that, although all individuals, on average, tended to disagree that the legal system is too harsh on individuals accused of crimes, stronger disagreement was evident among individuals who did not testify when the perpetrator received a lenient sentence and among testifiers when the perpetrator received a heavy sentence. In contrast, individuals who did not testify when the perpetrator received a heavy sentence tended to disagree the least. Perhaps these individuals, who had not testified, felt that the system had worked. Not only had they been sheltered from having to endure the stress of testifying, but the perpetrator was more severely punished.

The model was also significant when participants' disagreement with the statement, "The courts are too harsh on victims of crime" ($n = 167$), was considered, $F(9, 146) = 2.18, p < .05, R^2 = .12$. Experiencing more traumas, in addition to CSA and the perpetrator receiving a lenient sentence were both associated with stronger agreement that the courts are too harsh on victims.

Legal Risk and Number of Interviews

In our final analyses among only the target participants, we investigated whether participants' legal risk index scores and the number of interviews in which they had taken part during the former case were associated with their later general attitudes toward the legal system. As a reminder, the legal risk index reflects the number of adverse legal-case components to which participants were exposed (e.g., lack of corroborative evidence in the case, involvement in a concurrent dependency action, testifying). Again, number of interviews was not included in the legal risk index because of reduced n for this variable. Correlations were computed between participants' general

TABLE 20

LINEAR REGRESSIONS DEPICTING INDIVIDUAL, LEGAL, AND PROXIMAL PREDICTORS OF
PARTICIPANTS' GENERAL LEGAL ATTITUDES

	General Attitudes	
	Courts too Harsh on the Accused[e]	Courts too Harsh on Victims[e]
Predictor	Standardized Betas	
Step 1		
Age at Time 1[a]	.17*	−.11
Gender[b]	−.11	−.11
CBCL total T at Time 1	−.02	.04
Family risk index	−.06	.08
CSA risk index	.06	.02
Trauma risk index	.08	−.24**
Official arrest record	−.24**	.07
Step 2		
Testify status[c]	.06	−.03
Sentence severity[d]	.00	.17*
Step 3		
Age × testify	.01	—
CSA risk × testify	.07	—
Sentence × testify	.21*	—

Notes.—For the regression analysis predicting participants' disagreement that the courts are too harsh on individuals accused of crime, the overall model $F(12, 145) = 2.10$, $p < .05$, $R^2 = .15$; at step 1, $R^2 = .11$, $p < .05$, at step 2, $R^2\Delta = .00$, n.s., and at step 3, $R^2\Delta = .04$, $p < .10$. For the regression analysis predicting participants' disagreement that the courts are too harsh on victims, the model at step 2 $F(9, 146) = 2.18$, $p < .05$, $R^2 = .12$; at step 1, $R^2 = .09$, $p < .05$, at step 2, $R^2\Delta = .03$, $p < .10$; and at step 3, $R^2\Delta = .00$, n.s. CBCL, Child Behavior Checklist; CSA, child sexual abuse.
[a]Time 1 corresponds to the start of the original target CSA legal case.
[b]Gender was coded as 1 = male, 2 = female.
[c]Testify status was scored according to an ordinal scale (1 = did not testify, 3 = testified more than once).
[d]Sentence severity was scored according to an ordinal scale (0 = acquitted/case dismissed, 4 = department of corrections/prison).
[e]Responses scored on a scale from 1 = strongly agree to 4 = strongly disagree.
*$p < .05$.
**$p \leq .01$.

legal risk and number of interviews and the three general legal attitude measures (perceptions of the legal system's fairness and treatment of victims and defendants). Age, original CBCL T scores, and official arrest record were controlled statistically. None of the correlations was significant. Thus, neither the cumulative number of adverse components of the CSA legal case nor the number of interviews participants had endured were associated with general attitudes toward the legal system.

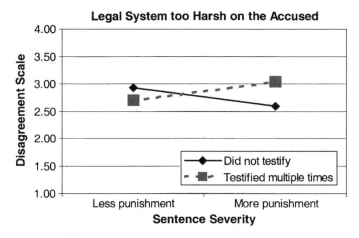

FIGURE 6.—Participants' level of disagreement with the statement, "The legal system is too harsh on individuals accused of crimes" as a function of sentence severity and testify status. Higher scores reflect greater disagreement with the statement, and the end points on the plot denote one standard deviation above and below the means for each predictor.

Summary

When general perceptions of the legal system were examined, age was related to long-term attitudes only in the legal involvement sample. Analyses of predictors of legal attitudes in only the legal involvement sample permitted us to take into account CSA and other risk factors that could not be considered in analyses that included the entire study sample. When these risk factors were considered concurrently, being an older adolescent at the time of a CSA legal case was associated with greater general feelings that the legal system is too lenient on defendants.

Participants' legal experiences were also related to their general legal attitudes in several important ways. First, CSA victims who did not testify rated the legal system as the most unfair, and significantly more so than did individuals with no CSA or CSA-related legal experiences. Second, among individuals who did not testify, those whose perpetrator received a lenient sentence disagreed more strongly than did those whose perpetrator received a severe sentence that the courts are too harsh on individuals accused of crimes. For the former individuals, experience had taught them otherwise. For the latter individuals, as mentioned, not only were they spared from having to testify, but the perpetrator was nonetheless punished harshly for the CSA. Third, individuals who testified multiple times when the perpetrator received a severe sentence also tended to disagree more strongly that the courts are too harsh on individuals accused of crimes. Based on the intensity of their involvement in the original case, these people may have felt that the defendant still got off easier than was warranted.

DO VICTIM/WITNESSES HOLD MORE NEGATIVE ATTITUDES THAN NONABUSED CONTROLS?

We had two main hypotheses concerning attitudinal differences between the legal involvement and control groups. First, because of the legal involvement group's greater contact with the criminal justice system as CSA victim/witnesses, we expected them to exhibit more negative feelings toward the legal system than the nonabused control group. Second, we expected age to interact with group status, such that individuals who were older at the time of the former legal case would exhibit the most negative legal attitudes.

In our first test of these hypotheses, we entered participants' mean unfairness ratings into a 3 (age at Time 1) × 3 (group status) ANCOVA with childhood CBCL T scores and participants' arrest record entered as covariates. Having an official arrest record (described in Chapter III) was also covaried. Again, legal experiences as a defendant may well influence legal attitudes. Also, the legal involvement sample had a greater number of prior arrests than the controls (see Chapter III).

A significant main effect of group status emerged, $F(2, 192) = 3.06$, $p < .05$, $\eta^2 = .03$. Planned comparisons provided partial support for our hypothesis: Participants who were involved in CSA legal cases but did not testify rated the legal system as significantly more unfair than did participants who had not been involved in the legal system as CSA victims, $F(1, 192) = 3.70$, $p < .05$ (Table 15). The testifiers' mean unfairness rating did not differ significantly from either the nontestifiers' or controls' mean rating. Because SES also differed across groups, a one-way group status ANCOVA was conducted including SES as an additional covariate, along with age, original CBCL T scores, and arrest record. The findings remained quite similar, although at a nonsignificant level, probably because of a loss of power given some missing data on the SES measure. Thus, in general, our findings suggest that, in the long term, children who did not take the stand later believed that the legal system is less fair.

In the original study, participants who were followed throughout their cases were asked after their case had ended, "Based on your experiences in this case, how would you rate the fairness of the criminal justice system overall?" A 2 (gender) × 2 (testifier vs. nontestifier) ANOVA revealed a trend indicating that, at the end of the 1992 study, girls felt that the system was less fair, $M = 2.24$, than boys, $M = 1.67$, $F(1, 60) = 3.45$, $p = .06$ (the scale ranged from 1 = very fair to 4 = very unfair). We examined whether a similar gender difference was evident, in the long term, in participants' mean unfairness responses (averaged across their current ratings of the unfairness of criminal courts, police practices, and juvenile courts). A 2 (gender) × 3 (group status) ANCOVA, with age at Time 1, CBCL T scores, and arrest record covaried, however, failed to reveal any significant effects involving gender. Thus, unlike in the 1992 study, gender differences in attitudes were not maintained in adolescents' and young adults' perceptions of the legal system's fairness.

Next, we conducted two 3 (age) × 3 (group status) ANCOVAs predicting participants' agreement with statements about the treatment of victims and defendants (Table 15). No significant age or group status effects emerged. Nor were any significant effects uncovered when the ANCOVAs were repeated substituting gender for age. Thus, unlike participants' unfairness ratings, which differed based on group status, participants' general attitudes toward the harshness of the courts' treatment of victims and defendants did not vary based on whether or not they had been involved or testified in a CSA-related legal case.

Summary

We investigated relations between participation in a CSA prosecution and later legal attitudes. Significant gender differences in general legal attitudes were not found. However, compared with control participants, victim/witnesses who did not have their day in court felt, years later, that the legal system is less fair. It is possible that the nontestifiers' attitudes were affected by their cases being more likely resolved through plea bargains, which then precluded the victims' need to testify, but which also resulted in less severe sentences for the accused. It is also possible that the victim/witnesses who did not testify felt more jaded about the legal system because they did not take the stand. The latter possibility is consistent with the procedural justice literature, which suggests that greater satisfaction with the legal system comes to those who more fully participate in it (e.g., Tompkins & Olejnik, 1978; Tyler & Lind, 2001).

VI. EMOTIONAL REACTIONS AT COURT IN RELATION TO CURRENT MENTAL HEALTH AND ATTITUDES

OVERVIEW

Did the child victim/witnesses' reactions at the courthouse or while on the witness stand predict their later outcomes? This question pertains to the final goal of our study: to investigate the role of children's emotional reactions at court in predicting their later mental health and legal attitudes. Extensive documentation from the 1992 study was available for participants who went to the courthouse expecting to testify and who actually testified. Included in this documentation was information regarding children's emotional distress while they were waiting to take the stand. Only a subset of the children went on to testify; the others went home (e.g., when a plea bargain was arranged at the last minute). While children testified, researchers observed the court proceedings and recorded children's emotional reactions (e.g., level of crying, overall negative response). Prior studies indicate that children's anticipation of testifying, in addition to their actual experiences while testifying, is related to their short-term adjustment (Berliner & Conte, 1995). We sought to determine whether such reactions also predicted the child victim/witnesses' long-term outcomes and whether such relations varied based on whether they went to court as preschoolers, in middle childhood, or as adolescents.

MEASURES

In the 1992 study, 110 children, ages 4–16 years, were interviewed while waiting at the courthouse to testify. Children were asked how they felt about being at court, about testifying, and about facing the defendant. The children responded by pointing to a four-point faces scale. Here, we were interested primarily in response to the request, "Point to the face that shows how you feel about going to court." This question was selected because all children for whom emotion data were available answered it (the other questions each had small numbers of missing data), and because it provides

94

an assessment of the children's overall anticipation of testifying. Also, children's feelings about being at court were moderately to strongly correlated with their feelings about talking to the judge and attorneys, and seeing the defendant in court, r's ranged from .42 to .67, p's < .001.

Sixty-three children, ages 4–17 years, eventually testified in their CSA cases. Researchers were able to observe 51 of them while they testified the first time. The researchers rated the children's overall emotional reactions on five-point scales (1 = very happy to 5 = very sad) while they answered the prosecutors', defense attorneys', and judges' questions (see Goodman et al., 1992, for details on scoring and reliability procedures). These ratings were moderately to strongly intercorrelated, r's > .46, and were combined into a single emotional reaction score. The researchers also rated whether the children cried while the prosecutor, defense attorney, and judge questioned them. From these ratings, a dichotomous "crying" score was computed to reflect whether each child cried at any point during her/his testimony.

Of the 110 individuals from the 1992 study sample who provided ratings of their feelings about going to court, 82 (74% females) completed Phase 1 of the current study. Of the 51 individuals who were observed in the 1992 study when they actually testified in court, 41 (83% females) completed Phase 1 of the current study. To determine the representativeness of the current sample, comparisons were made in the emotional ratings at court between participants who completed the current study (n's = 82 and 41, for before court and while testifying, respectively) versus individuals from the 1992 study who did not (n's = 28 and 10, respectively). No significant differences emerged.

HOW DOES CHILDREN'S AGE WHILE AT THE COURTHOUSE RELATE TO THEIR EMOTIONAL REACTIONS?

Several associations between participants' age at the time of their court case and their emotional reactions at the courthouse were reported in the 1992 study. Older children were more anxious about having to testify and were more emotional in court than younger children, a pattern that stands in contrast to developmental literature revealing age-related decreases in children's distress responses to salient personal experiences (Goodman, Quas, Batterman-Faunce, Riddlesberger, & Kuhn, 1994; Merritt, Ornstein, & Spicker, 1994; Peterson & Bell, 1998). Here, we examined whether developmental differences in emotional reactions were related to long-term outcomes. First, however, we investigated whether similar age-related differences in emotional reactions were evident among participants who completed the current study. Results obtained with the current sample were virtually identical to those obtained with the entire 1992 sample.

95

The current study participants' pre-court ratings of how they felt about being at court were entered into a one-way age-at-court (4–6, 7–11, and 12–17 years) ANCOVA (Table 21). Participants' CBCL T scores were entered as a covariate to control for possible effects of preprosecution behavioral functioning on children's distress responses at court. The age categories reflect participants' age when they were awaiting their hearing or trial, rather than, as in analyses reported in the prior chapters, their age at the start of the legal case. Although the two are strongly correlated, because the length of the legal cases and the number of continuances varied, not all participants were in the same age categories when the legal case began and when they actually testified. The main effect of age was significant, $F(2, 77) = 8.39, p = .001, \eta^2 = .18$. Participants between the ages of 4 and 6 years while waiting at court reported at the time feeling slightly positive about being there. Both the older age groups (ages 7–11 years and 12–17 years) reported negative feelings about being at court. Planned comparisons revealed that the latter two age groups' means were significantly higher (reflecting greater negativity) than was the younger age group's mean, F's$(1, 77) > 6.18, p$'s $< .01$. Again, this age trend is surprising in light of a large body of research indicating age-related decreases in children's emotional responses to stressful events, including as measured in terms of children's anticipatory reactions to impending stressors

TABLE 21

CHILDREN'S EMOTIONAL REACTIONS WHILE WAITING TO TESTIFY AND WHILE TESTIFYING IN COURT

	Age at Court		
Emotional Reaction	4–6 years	7–11 years	12–17 years
		Pre-Court	
Feelings about being at court[a]	1.91 (1.30)	2.74 (.93)	3.08 (.72)
	$n = 11$	$n = 19$	$n = 51$
		In-Court	
Mean emotional reaction[b]	2.78 (.79)	3.52 (.80)	3.68 (.73)
	$n = 9$	$n = 14$	$n = 18$
Percent who cried while testifying	0%	50%	39%
	$n = 6$	$n = 12$	$n = 18$

Notes.—Both the pre-court and in-court ratings were collected during Goodman et al.'s (1992) original study in which researchers accompanied children to court and observed children while they waited and as they testified. Only participants who also completed the current study are included in these means.
[a]Participants' self-reported feelings about being at court were measured according to a four-point face scale rating system (1 = very positive to 4 = very negative).
[b]Participants' emotional reactions in court were measured according to a mean composite score, created by averaging the researcher's ratings of the child's emotional reaction at proscribed times while testifying (i.e., during direct, cross-examination, etc.) on a five-point scale (1 = very happy to 5 = very sad).

(e.g., Goodman et al., 1994). However, because children's legal understanding generally increases with age (e.g., Davis et al., 2005; Saywitz et al., 1990), and the demands placed on children by the legal system often increase with age (Goodman et al., 1992), the older children may have better understood the potentially traumatic nature of the upcoming testimony and hence reacted more negatively about being at court.

Similar analyses were conducted to investigate associations between age and emotional reactions in the smaller group of children ($n = 41$) who eventually testified in the case. Their emotional reaction score was entered as the dependent measure in a one-way age group ANCOVA, with CBCL T score covaried. A significant effect of age, $F(2, 37) = 4.39$, $p < .05$, $\eta^2 = .20$, revealed a similar pattern: The youngest participants displayed significantly less negativity than participants who were 7–11 and 12–17, F's $(1, 37) = 5.56$, p's $< .05$. Specifically, whereas none of the participants who were ages 4–6 cried during the direct examination, half of the participants who were ages 7–11 years and slightly under half of those who were ages 12–17 years cried (Table 21). Again, the older children's greater knowledge about and anticipation of the stressful situation may have increased their anxiety while testifying. Moreover, as reported in the 1992 study, older children underwent longer questioning than younger children, and defense attorneys and prosecutors were less supportive of the older than of the younger children while they testified. Each of these factors may have contributed to the age-related increases in children's negative emotional reactions both before and during courtroom testimony, reactions that go against commonly observed age-related changes in overt distress to naturalistic stressors (e.g., Dahlquist, Power, Cox, & Fernbach, 1994; Goodman, Hirschman, Hepps, & Rudy, 1991).

HOW DO EARLIER EMOTIONAL REACTIONS RELATE TO LATER MENTAL HEALTH?

Given the potential significance of participants' childhood emotional reactions for their later mental health, it was important to determine whether these reactions, alone or in conjunction with age at the time of the case, predicted their later trauma-related symptoms or general mental health. We hypothesized that greater distress before and while testifying would be associated with poorer mental health later on. We further hypothesized that this association would be particularly robust among individuals who were young (e.g., preschool-age) when they appeared at court. We tested these hypotheses in analyses that were computed separately for individuals who waited at the courthouse to testify and individuals who actually testified.

First, however, we conducted one-way ANCOVAs on the PTSD, DES, and BSI scores and MANCOVAs on the scores for the TSI sexual problems and defensive avoidance subscales, the YABCL internalizing and externalizing scales, and the YASR internalizing and externalizing scales among three groups of legal involvement participants: those who did not testify but who went to court waiting and expecting to do so, those who testified in the former case, and those who never went to court. With age at the start of the legal case and original CBCL T scores controlled statistically, significant group differences emerged only for defensive avoidance, $F(2, 164) = 3.10$, $p = .05$, $\eta^2 = .03$. Consistent with the findings reported in prior chapters concerning testifying and later mental health, individuals who actually testified, $M = 9.15$, $n = 45$, but also individuals who went to court expecting to testify but never did, $M = 9.88$, $n = 33$, reported higher levels of defensive avoidance than did individuals who never went to court, $M = 6.55$, $n = 91$.

Participants' Pre-Court Anticipation of Testifying

Regression analyses were conducted to test the predictions concerning participants' pre-court emotional reactions. Dependent measures included the trauma-specific measures (TSI sexual problems, TSI defensive avoidance, DES dissociative tendencies, PTSD symptoms) and general mental health measures (caregiver-completed YABCL internalizing and externalizing scales, BSI mean, and YASR internalizing and externalizing scales). In the regressions, participants' age while waiting at the courthouse, CBCL T scores, and feelings about being at court were entered on the first step. The interaction between participants' age and their feelings about being at court was entered on the second step to test our prediction that, among highly distressed individuals, those who were young when they were waiting to testify would exhibit the highest level of later mental health problems.

Among the trauma-specific symptom analyses, the model predicting participants' current defensive avoidance symptoms was significant, $F(3, 60) = 3.59$, $p < .05$, $R^2 = .15$ (the $R^2\Delta$ at step 2 was nonsignificant). Participants' pre-court feelings about being at court were significantly related to their defensive avoidance symptoms: Greater negativity while waiting at the courthouse predicted higher levels of defensive avoidance symptoms years later, $\beta = .40$, $p < .001$.

We next examined participants' later general mental health in relation to their emotion ratings provided in childhood while waiting at the courthouse. The models predicting participants' YABCL internalizing and externalizing symptoms were both significant. For internalizing symptoms, $F(4, 41) = 6.29$, $p < .001$, overall $R^2 = .38$; step 1 $R^2\Delta = .27$ and step 2 $R^2\Delta = .11$, p's $\leq .01$. Significant predictors included participants' CBCL T

scores, their pre-court feelings about being at court, and the age × feelings interaction. Higher CBCL T scores and feeling more negative about being at court while waiting to testify were positively associated with later caregiver-reported internalizing symptoms, β's > .40, p's < .05. The significant interaction ($\beta = .39$, $p < .05$), however, indicated that the age effect was being driven by participants who were older when they waited at court (Figure 7). Among participants who were younger, how they felt before court was unrelated to their later internalizing symptoms.

Results of the model predicting externalizing symptoms, $F(3, 42) = 5.22$, $p < .01$, $R^2 = .27$ (the $R^2\Delta$ at step 2, $p < .06$; the interaction β was nonsignificant) were consistent with analyses reported in Chapter IV predicting externalizing symptoms in the entire legal involvement sample. Among the subset of individuals who waited at court to testify, being younger, $\beta = .30$, $p < .06$, and having a higher original CBCL T score, $\beta = .41$, $p < .01$, were associated with more symptoms years later, although the age finding fell just short of statistical significance. (The statistical power was reduced because of the relatively small number of participants included in the analysis.)

When participants' mean on the BSI items from the Phase 1 interview were examined, the model was significant, $F(3, 76) = 4.02$, $p = .01$, $R^2 = .14$ (step 2 $R^2\Delta = .02$, n.s.). Among individuals who waited at court to testify, being younger while waiting was associated with higher levels of later symptoms, $\beta = -.26$, $p < .05$, as was having a higher CBCL T score before the prosecution began, $\beta = .32$, $p < .05$. Finally, neither of the models pre-

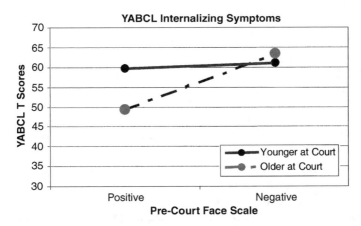

FIGURE 7.—Young Adult Behavior Checklist (YABCL) internalizing T scores as a function of participants' age while waiting at the courthouse and their feelings about being in court, as reported at the time according to a 4-point face scale rating system. Higher scores reflect greater symptomatology, and the end points on the plot denote one standard deviation above and below the means for each predictor.

dicting participants' self-reported internalizing and externalizing symptoms on the YASR was significant at either step.

Overall, greater distress while waiting to testify was associated with mental problems years later. Moreover, individuals who were younger at the time of the legal case, including when they waited at the courthouse to testify, had higher levels of externalizing behavior problems. However, older children who were particularly distressed while waiting at court to testify had higher levels of internalizing problems.

Participants' In-Court Reactions and Later Mental Health

The smaller sample size precluded us from conducting regressions to examine associations between participants' emotional reactions while testifying and later adjustment. We instead correlated participants' mean emotional reaction while testifying and the dichotomous crying variable with the trauma and general mental health measures, with participants' age at the time of testifying and CBCL T scores partialled. None of the correlations between participants' emotional mood and mental health was significant. However, crying during the direct examination was associated with later sexual problems, $r = .39$, $df = 28$, and with higher caregiver-reported internalizing symptoms, $r = .49$, $df = 21$, p's $< .05$. Having cried was also marginally related to later self-reported externalizing symptoms, $r = .32$, $df = 28$, $p < .10$. Thus, even 12 years after testifying in court, and even with age and preprosecution behavioral adjustment controlled statistically, being more distressed on the witness stand, as indicated by crying when testifying, was associated with adverse outcomes.

HOW DO EARLIER EMOTIONAL REACTIONS AT COURT RELATE TO LATER LEGAL ATTITUDES?

Our final set of analyses concerned relations between participants' emotional reactions while at court and their later legal attitudes. We expected higher distress to be associated with more negative feelings later on, especially feelings about the former case. We further hypothesized that participants' emotional reactions would interact with age at the time of the trial to predict current negative attitudes, with the oldest individuals who were also distressed reporting the most negative feelings about the case. In the analyses reported below, we first considered attitudes about the legal system among individuals who were assessed, in childhood, while waiting to testify. We then considered later attitudes as a function of emotional reactions of individuals who actually took the stand in childhood.

Participants' Pre-Court Anticipation of Testifying and Current Attitudes

In our first tests of these hypotheses, we conducted regression analyses to determine if participants' pre-court emotional ratings predicted their later perceptions of the effects of the former CSA case on their lives and their current satisfaction with the outcome of the case. (Only participants who disclosed the target case were included in these analyses.) We then conducted similar analyses to investigate whether participants' pre-court ratings also predicted later perceptions of the legal system's fairness and the appropriateness of its treatment of crime victims and of individuals accused of crimes and treatment of crime victims. As in the regression analyses examining mental health outcomes described earlier, predictors included participants' age while waiting to testify, original CBCL T scores, and pre-court ratings of how they felt about being at court on step 1, and the age × feelings interaction on step 2. None of these analyses yielded significant results.

Participants' In-Court Reactions and Current Attitudes

Next, partial correlations were computed to examine whether participants' emotional reactions while testifying were related to their later attitudes. Age when participants testified and original CBCL T scores were statistically controlled. When participants' mean emotional reaction while testifying score was correlated with their current ratings of the effects of the former case on their lives and satisfaction with the former case, no significant associations were found. Nor was participants' mean emotional reaction while testifying related to their general perceptions of the legal system's fairness, treatment of defendants, and treatment of victims. Having cried while testifying, however, was associated with participants' current attitudes. Having cried predicted feeling later that the CSA case had a more negative effect on the participants' lives, $r = .38$, $p = .05$, $df = 26$. (The correlation between having cried and perceiving the legal system as unfair was relatively substantial but fell short of significance, $r = .31$, $p < .10$, $df = 30$.) Thus, participants' visible distress while testifying was associated with more negative feelings about effects of the legal case on their lives and also, to a certain extent, with feeling more negative later about the legal system generally.[3]

SUMMARY

Together, analyses of participants' pre-court and in-court emotional reactions produced a number of important results. First, a somewhat surprising, although interpretable result concerns age-related differences in children's distress reactions at court: Older rather than younger individuals were more distressed, both before they testified (as reported by the participants themselves) and while they testified (as rated by the researchers). In medical contexts, children's overt distress reactions often decrease with age (e.g., Dahlquist et al., 1994). Yet, in the legal context, older children are treated more harshly, are at times less likely to be believed, and are more cognizant of the implications of their participation for the case (Bottoms & Goodman, 1992; Goodman et al., 1992), all of which probably contribute to their increased distress both in anticipation of and while actually testifying.

Second, participants' emotional reactions were related to their mental health years later, in part as we hypothesized. Because we statistically controlled for pre-prosecution behavioral adjustment, our findings hold over and above the child victim/witnesses' mental health problems as reported at the start of the prosecution. Feeling more negative about having to testify, regardless of whether the participant actually did testify, was associated with higher levels of defensive avoidance years after the courthouse visit. In addition, among participants who were older while they waited to testify, feeling more negative about court was related to having internalizing symptoms later in life. Thus, consistent with Berliner and Conte's (1995) study of short-term consequences of legal involvement on CSA victims, the anticipation of testifying in a CSA legal case had implications for long-term mental health, especially among individuals who were older when they went to court. Similar findings were obtained when participants' actual distress responses while testifying were considered. Having cried was related to later sexual problems and caregiver-reported internalizing symptoms. Overall, even though testifying itself may have taken place only on one particular day, the anticipation of this day, as well as individuals' emotional reactions to it, appear to have affected mental health in the long term. It should be kept in mind that we analyzed children's emotional reactions to their first court appearance. Sample size was too small to analyze their responses when they testified for the second or third time, experiences that may also have influenced the individuals' long-term functioning.

Third, when participants' legal attitudes were considered, relatively few significant findings were obtained. However, the few significant effects again suggested that being more distressed while testifying was associated with more negative feelings regarding the effects of the legal case on their lives.

Overall, these analyses underscore the need for continued scientific investigation of the relations among age, emotional reactions, and long-term consequences for child victim/witnesses. Such investigations will provide much-needed information about how children's emotional reactions to a confusing and challenging life event vary with development, and how these varying reactions relate to long-term outcomes.

NOTE

3. In the current study, some participants were siblings (e.g., two siblings were involved in a case against a parent). Additionally, in some cases, one perpetrator had been accused of molesting several of the participants when they were children (e.g., several neighborhood children were involved in a case against a neighbor who sexually assaulted them). Because of resulting concerns about violation of statistical independence, the main regression analyses in each of the three results chapters were reconducted first by randomly selecting one of the siblings per family (the number of participants omitted per analysis ranged from five to eight), and second, by randomly selecting one child per perpetrator (the number of participants omitted per analysis ranged from 12 to 25). These analyses confirmed the significant findings and/or trends reported in the main text of this *Monograph*. A few effects reported in the main text became nonsignificant, most likely due to loss of power. However, trends remained in the same direction as those reported.

VII. GENERAL DISCUSSION

Goodman et al.'s (1992) study of the immediate and short-term consequences of testifying in criminal court revealed that legal involvement is stressful for many children and can increase or maintain child and adolescent psychopathology, at least in the short term. The results were cited in the U.S. Supreme Court's decision that face-to-face confrontation may not always be warranted in child sexual assault cases, because it can inflict psychological damage to the child and interfere with the child's communication of her or his memories (Maryland v. Craig, 1990). Even before the 1992 study, some researchers had claimed that testifying in CSA trials could be so harmful to children as to constitute a form of "secondary victimization," leading to psychological injury independent of the crime itself (e.g., Glaser & Spencer, 1990; Katz & Mazur, 1979). However, whether testifying could be appropriately conceptualized as a stressor (i.e., an event objectively threatening to an individual's health or well-being; Grant, Compas, Stuhlmacher, Thurm, McMahon, & Halpert, 2003) was, from a scientific standpoint, unclear. Findings from the 1992 study indicated that even after crucial variables related to the abuse (e.g., abuse severity) and the legal case (e.g., case outcome) were taken into account, testifying—especially repeatedly—was in fact stressful for many children and was related to poorer mental health in the short-term as measured with by CBCL (Achenbach, 1994; Achenbach & Edelbrock, 1981).

What was not known, based on the 1992 study, was whether adverse effects of criminal court involvement persist over time. By reassessing the former victim/witnesses and adding a nonabused control group, we were able to investigate, for the first time, how several important outcomes relate to having endured a stressful, lengthy, confusing, and challenging experience—legal involvement—years before, in childhood. We were also able to determine whether certain features of children's legal experiences reduce the long-term adverse effects of CSA or create additional traumas with which the already victimized children must cope.

104

Our investigation included several kinds of predictors. At the individual level, we considered most notably age, but also gender and pre-prosecution mental health. Other predictors, at the proximal level, included legal involvement, characteristics of the CSA, family stressors, and other adverse life experiences. We approached our study from a developmental perspective, considering that the effects of childhood stress might differ as a function of a child's developmental level at the time of the stressor (e.g., Egeland, Carlson, & Sroufe, 1993).

Our findings indicate that children's long-term mental health and attitudes following CSA-related legal involvement were affected by their age when the legal case began. However, the associations between age and the two types of outcomes varied. When mental health functioning was considered, being younger was often related to poorer outcomes. When legal attitudes were considered, being older was often related to more negative feelings. The two outcomes were also related to having testified in court, although these associations often depended on other case and abuse characteristics. For example, testifying was associated with increased risk for adverse mental health outcomes, particularly when children testified about highly invasive abuse. However, under certain conditions (i.e., when the perpetrator was acquitted or received a lenient sentence), *not* testifying was also associated with adverse outcomes. Thus, we cannot say that testifying was uniformly "bad" and not testifying was uniformly "good" for child victim/witnesses. Instead, a complex combination of factors predicted long-term mental health and attitudinal outcomes. We turn to this complexity next.

PREDICTORS OF LONG-TERM OUTCOMES

According to multilevel-transactional developmental theories and the research such theories have inspired (e.g., Bronfenbrenner, 1979; Masten & Wright, 1998), outcomes following exposure to stressful life events are influenced by variables at the individual, proximal, and distal system levels. Factors of central interest in our study included participants' age when their legal case began and the nature of their experiences with the legal system. These two factors were considered within the broader context of other individual and proximal level risk factors that might affect mental health and attitudes over time. Each of these influences—development, legal involvement, and domains of risk—is discussed in turn next.

Developmental Level

The first primary question addressed in our study concerned how children's age or developmental level at the time of their participation in a

105

CSA legal case relates to their later mental health and attitudes about the legal system. We hypothesized that the associations between age and outcomes would vary depending on which type of outcome was being considered, an expectation supported by previous research. Studies of children's reactions to trauma, including CSA, suggest that being especially young (e.g., preschool-age) when a trauma takes place is particularly harmful for later mental health (e.g., Egeland et al., 2002; Finkelhor, 1979; Sanchez et al., 2001). Based on this literature, we predicted that young children who testified repeatedly would be at the greatest risk for later psychological problems, because of both the earlier experience of CSA and the stress of having to testify multiple times about it.

In contrast, when legal attitudes were considered, we expected being older at the time of the legal case to predict more negative later attitudes toward the legal system. Older children have a better understanding of the legal system (e.g., Davis et al., 2005) and a greater appreciation of the implications of their legal case for themselves, their family, other potential victims, and the defendant (Cashmore & Bussey, 1989; Melton & Berliner, 1992; Saywitz, 1989; Warren-Leubecker et al., 1989). Moreover, older children are treated more harshly when they testify in court (i.e., they are cross-examined more harshly; Goodman et al., 1992). Each of these factors was expected to contribute to older children's more negative feelings about the legal system and about their particular case.

Our hypotheses were partially supported, with younger age when the legal case began predicting higher levels of later externalizing problems, and older age when the legal case began predicting greater disagreement that the courts are too harsh on individuals accused of crime. Age rarely interacted with participants' testifying status, however, suggesting that age at the time of the prosecution per se did not differentially predict long-term outcomes for testifiers versus nontestifiers. Instead, direct associations between age and outcomes were generally observed.

With respect to mental health, the fact that younger age at the time of the case was associated with higher levels of later externalizing symptoms may have several possible explanations. Initially, young children may not fully appreciate the inappropriateness of a perpetrator's behavior or the nature and purpose of the legal case. Moreover, they may not attribute moral meaning to their experiences (e.g., Cederborg & Lamb, 2004; Celano, 1992; Spaccarelli, 1994). Over time, however, this lack of initial understanding may contribute to increasingly negative feelings. Young children may also be confused about their legal case and court appearance and less able to cope with the demands they encounter in court. Their lack of understanding may be replaced over time by growing anger and resentment, which contributes to later poor adjustment. Such a possibility is exemplified by one participant, who was age 6 years when the legal case began. She explained, "I was very young . . . It was confusing and shameful because of the "revealment." I was too young to know what was going on."

In general, adolescents in the sample of participants who waited at the courthouse in anticipation of testifying reported more pre-court anxiety than their younger counterparts. Yet, as a group, adolescents overall did not evince higher levels of later externalizing or internalizing symptoms. Instead, only adolescents who reported negative feelings about being at court were at increased risk for later mental health problems, specifically, internalizing symptoms. Adolescents who reported positive feelings about being at court had the lowest levels of later internalizing symptoms. Feelings about being at court among the younger participants were unrelated to later internalizing symptoms. Perhaps individuals who were both older when they waited at the courthouse to testify and reported feeling positive about it at the time were empowered by their participation in the legal case, recognizing and accepting their important contribution to the legal process. Positive situational appraisals and feelings of control have been associated with better outcomes in a variety of stressful settings (Lazarus, 1991; Thibaut & Walker, 1975). To the extent that feeling positive about being at court reflects a sense of control, especially among older child victim/witnesses who understand their role at court, such feelings may contribute to successful coping, thereby reducing adverse long-term outcomes.

When age-related differences in legal attitudes emerged, being older at the time of the legal case was associated with more negative general feelings about the legal system, specifically disagreeing that the system is too harsh on individuals accused of crime. It should be noted that case outcomes were no less severe among the older participants, so age differences in feelings about the treatment of defendants are not simply the result of differential treatment of the defendant in the former CSA legal case. Instead, we believe that the older participants' harsher treatment in court, combined with their greater understanding of the meaning and implications of the legal decisions (Block et al., 2005; Saywitz et al., 1990; Whitcomb et al., 1991) may have led to their more negative attitudes.

In contrast to the above finding, when attitudes were examined over time, participants who were particularly young at the time of the legal case became less negative in their attitudes, whereas participants who were older when they went to court did not exhibit significant attitude change. On the one hand, the younger children in the 1992 study probably had limited understanding of the legal process and were not able to engage in complex reasoning about the legal system, justice, and their participation. Younger children may thus have felt the most negative and confused after the original case ended. On the other hand, however, at the time of the original study, some caregivers assisted children in answering the original study questionnaires. Such assistance was likely most important for the youngest children, many of whom were unable to read the questions themselves. Caregivers' own feelings may have influenced the children's initial responses. Such a pattern could have led to the young children's especially high reports of negative feelings at the end of the 1992 study relative to the reports of the older children at that time and relative to all individuals' current reports.

Two other developmental findings are noteworthy. First, the nature of children's legal experiences varied with age. Younger children were more likely to experience repeated continuances, lack of maternal support, lack of corroborative evidence, the defendant being acquitted/case being dropped, and the child having to testify repeatedly. These experiences contributed to younger children's higher scores on our composite measure of legal risk. Yet, older children were interviewed more frequently about the alleged abuse, and repeated interviews were associated with increased mental health problems. Older children were also more likely to go to court expecting to testify than were younger children, even though age differences did not emerge in whether children in fact testified. It is important to understand how these characteristics of the legal process may influence relations between children's age and their reactions to legal involvement. Our study represents the first step in this regard, but additional research with larger and more diverse samples is needed.

Second, when participants' emotional reactions at the courthouse (both while waiting to testify and while testifying) were examined, as mentioned, older rather than younger participants were more distressed. This finding makes sense for individuals who testified because the older children were in fact questioned longer, and both the prosecutor and defense attorney were less supportive in their questioning of older victim/witnesses. The younger children, in contrast, were often provided with more support and assistance while testifying. An example of this assistance is provided by one of our participants, who was describing her experience testifying in court as a pre-schooler, "We went to the courthouse, and a room had toys. The legal district attorney came, and everyone was gentle and caring . . ."

Yet, even among the larger sample of individuals waiting at the court-house but who did not necessarily testify, older children reported feeling more negative about being at court than did younger children. Thus, although research suggests that greater knowledge about impending stressors reduces distress (e.g., Nathanson & Saywitz, 2003; Oran, 1989; Sattar & Bull, 1996), within our study, the older children, who presumably were more knowledgeable about the legal system and their own legal case, were more anxious and distressed, both before and while testifying. Of course, these results do not suggest that children should be kept naïve to legal involvement as a means of reducing their immediate distress. Instead, these results highlight the need for interventions to reduce distress among all

108

children, including for those children who are old enough to understand and evaluate the legal process, their role in that process, and the significance of the case and its outcome.

Finally, it is important to mention that our indicator of development in the present study was chronological age, which may not reflect children's true developmental level. Within a given chronological age, children's cognitive, social, and emotional skills vary considerably. Additionally, regardless of chronological age, children who are developmentally advanced (e.g., as assessed by measures of intelligence or academic performance) are better equipped to understand the legal system and perform better on legally relevant tasks (e.g., competency to stand trial; Goldstein, Condie, Kalbeitzer, Osman, & Geier, 2003; Redlich, Silverman, & Steiner, 2003). These developmental differences could affect how children react to and cope with legal involvement, as well as how they understand and think about their experiences over time. Given that developmental level is a potentially significant moderator of the consequences of childhood trauma, it will be imperative in future research to obtain more precise measures of children's developmental level. By doing so, outcomes for child victim/witnesses in relation to their development can be further clarified.

Legal Involvement

The second central question addressed in our study concerned the long-term consequences of specific legal experiences for child victim/witnesses. Of primary interest was the relation between testifying in court and participants' later mental health and legal attitudes. We also examined the role of other components of the victim/witnesses' legal experiences, such as the number of interviews, children's emotional reaction while testifying, and the outcome of the case.

A number of findings confirmed results of former studies (e.g., Runyan, as cited in Whitcomb et al., 1991; Sas, 1993) and revealed that testifying in court, especially repeatedly, was associated with negative mental health consequences. One participant, for example, explained: "I had to testify in court in front of the defendant and point him out. It was very difficult . . . I also had to sit away from my mother and not have eye contact with her while being questioned by the attorneys—very difficult also . . . I had to explain the details in court in front of everyone!" First, testifying more frequently was associated with higher levels of internalizing symptoms in adolescents and young adults. Second, having testified in a case involving more invasive sexual abuse (e.g., long-lasting abuse, perpetrated by a parental figure, involving penetration) predicted higher levels of self-reported sexual problems. These results are quite noteworthy in that the adverse effects of testifying were apparent 12 years (on average) after this particular stressful

109

event had taken place. Thus, testifying may exert an influence on long-term functioning both independently and in combination with particularly severe CSA (Kendall-Tackett et al., 1993; Sas, 1991).

Third, participants who testified repeatedly and whose cases resulted in a severe sentence for the perpetrator had higher internalizing and externalizing symptoms relative to individuals who did not testify and whose cases resulted in a similarly severe sentence. We speculate that the distress associated with repeatedly recounting sexual abuse experiences in open court may have offset any positive mental health consequences that could have resulted from the positive case outcome, at least in terms of the sentence being more severe. In contrast, participants who were spared from having to testify and whose cases nevertheless resulted in a severe sentence for the perpetrator may have felt that, not only were they protected but their allegations were vindicated. Thus, they may have been better able to cope with the abuse. One participant, age 6 years when her case began, explicitly mentioned not testifying, in conjunction with the perpetrator's sentence, as one of the positive consequences of her legal experiences: "That he was put in jail . . . he was sentenced . . . and I didn't have to testify."

Finally, among the subset of individuals identified in the 1992 study as improving in behavioral adjustment in the short term, those who had not testified evinced better current mental health functioning than did those who had testified. Additionally, even though some testifiers had improved in the short term, their current mental health functioning appeared no better than that of testifiers (and nontestifiers) who had not improved in the short term. The generalizability of the findings may be limited, however, because these analyses included a particularly small sample and the improver/nonimprover distinction was based on potentially small changes in Child Behavior Checklist (CBCL) scores during the original 1992 study. Nonetheless, the pattern is consistent with analyses of our larger sample in revealing the importance of testifying repeatedly as a predictor of adverse mental health outcomes that persist into adulthood.

Many stressful and traumatizing events occur throughout people's lives. The probability of experiencing several forms of trauma is even higher for those who have been exposed to violence as children (e.g., Arata, 2002). In this context, it is striking that a circumscribed episode, or the experiences associated with that episode, still predicts important outcomes more than a decade later. These findings suggest that testifying does not simply upset children, as was documented by Goodman et al. (1992), but may be associated with their adjustment at a deeper level. Overall then, our findings suggest that, *under certain conditions*, recounting sexual abuse repeatedly in open court may help solidify a trajectory of poor mental health functioning, as measured both via trauma-related symptomatology and general mental health problems.

Yet, there were certain circumstances under which *not* testifying was associated with negative long-term outcomes. For instance, participants who did not testify in cases involving less severe CSA (e.g., extrafamilial abuse involving minimal sexual contact) later reported higher levels of defensive avoidance. Anger or resentment at not having one's day in court or perhaps feeling that one should have done more to help the case, together with active attempts to avoid thinking about the experience, could lead to increased defensive avoidance behaviors.

Not testifying was also associated with more negative attitudes toward the legal system: Nontestifiers perceived the legal system to be less fair than did the control participants. Additionally, individuals who did not testify and whose cases resulted in a lenient sentence for the perpetrator felt that the legal system was not harsh enough on individuals accused of crimes. Experience has taught them otherwise. Perhaps participants who testified now have a sense that they did all they could in the case, regardless of the outcome, whereas participants who did not testify, at least when the perpetrator was not punished, resent or lament not having testified and feel that their testimony might have helped secure a conviction or a harsher sentence. Such feelings could lead to long-term negative attitudes about the legal system's responsiveness.

Perceptions of justice are closely linked with perceptions of fairness (Lind & Tyler, 1988; Tyler & Folger, 1980; Tyler & Lind, 1992). As such, participants' satisfaction with their case and with the legal system in general may rest more with their perceptions of how well justice was served than with the level of psychological discomfort they experienced in the courtroom. Because testifying provides the opportunity to take an active role in the prosecution, it may contribute to individuals' beliefs about the importance of their participation and thus contribute to their sense of procedural justice. Our results are consistent with the hypothesis that testifying may increase participants' feelings of control over the legal process. Thus, individuals who did not testify may not have felt that they had a "say" in the case, or an opportunity to publicly tell their story. Lack of control may well reduce individuals' perceptions that the legal system is fair (e.g., Folger, 1977; Tyler, 1988).

Several other legal case characteristics, in addition to testifying, emerged as significant predictors of participants' later mental health and legal attitudes. In particular, consistent with our hypotheses and with Sas's (1993) study of child victims' reactions to criminal court involvement 3 years after the verdicts occurred, the perpetrator's sentence was significantly related to participants' current attitudes: Less severe sentences predicted more negative feelings about the former legal case, the outcome, and about having testified or not testified. Participants often directly linked the outcome to their current feelings in their narrative descriptions of their experiences: "The lack of conviction gave me a negative attitude toward the legal system" and "the sexual abuse was not punished to my satisfaction."

Also, in the analyses predicting long-term functioning among testifiers and nontestifiers who had versus had not improved in the short-term, lack of maternal support predicted greater internalizing symptoms. These findings are consistent with a large body of research on risk and protective factors following exposure to childhood trauma, including CSA and legal involvement (e.g., Conte & Berliner, 1988; Elder & Caspi, 2000; Elder & Conger, 2000; Rutter, 1971). It should be noted, however, that maternal unsupportiveness could reflect disbelief of the allegations, anger or resentment toward the child for disclosing the abuse, or the mother's own reaction to her child's abuse. In any case, and in light of research revealing the importance of primary caregivers' support for children's development, further investigation into the sources of parents' supportiveness and the role of their support in the legal process is clearly needed.

Domains of Risk

In our analyses, we also considered characteristics of the child (e.g., gender and preprosecution mental health) and characteristics proximal to the child (e.g., exposure to additional life traumas, adverse family experiences, and CSA invasiveness). Our study is the first to examine such characteristics, in conjunction with children's age and legal experiences, as predictors of mental health and legal attitudes following participation as a victim in a criminal case.

First, considering individual characteristics, we had hypothesized that gender would interact with participants' legal involvement status to predict internalizing versus externalizing symptoms. This hypothesis was not supported. In fact, few gender differences were evident in our study. In one exception, gender was related to long-term attitudes. As was reported in the 1992 study, females expressed somewhat more negative feelings about the legal case compared with males. Although sentence severity (which was also related to participants' satisfaction with the case) did not differ by gender, females were subjected to more invasive abuse (i.e., that involved a parental figure perpetrator, took place over several years, and involved penetration). It is possible that their negative perceptions of the case stem more from the abuse per se than from the resulting legal experience. Nevertheless, our findings are consistent with research revealing women's proclivities when evaluating victims of sexual assault and legal cases involving claims of CSA (Bottoms, 1993). Our findings demonstrate that these proclivities extend to female victims' attitudes toward their own case.

112

Second, participants' preprosecution mental health, as measured via the CBCL at the start of the legal case, predicted subsequent mental health problems. Thus, individuals who had behavior problems initially, perhaps because of the abuse or because of other related family dysfunction, continued to exhibit problems later, both as reported by participants (i.e., the BSI-item subset) and by their caregivers (i.e., YABCL). These results confirm a larger body of research concerning mental health functioning over time in demonstrating the importance of early mental health as a predictor of long-term outcomes (e.g., Messer et al., 2004; Rudd et al., 2004), even across different types of measures and reporters.

Third, proximal factors (i.e., exposure to additional traumas, adverse familial experiences, and characteristics of the CSA itself) predicted participants' mental health and, to some extent, legal attitudes. In our study, few abuse characteristics directly predicted long-term outcomes; instead, participants' abuse experiences, as reflected in their CSA risk scores, interacted with whether and how often participants testified in the legal case to predict particular outcomes. The implications of these interactions were discussed earlier. Here, we simply note that the lack of direct association between CSA characteristics and long-term outcomes does not in any way imply that CSA is without adverse effects. The design of our study did not permit us to examine the effects of CSA per se. Instead, because we included a CSA-plus-legal-involvement sample that varied in the extent of such involvement, we were able to examine predictors of outcomes in CSA victims following their involvement in a criminal prosecution.

Finally, it is worth mentioning one other proximal level factor that predicted current legal attitudes, namely having a criminal arrest history. Among our sample of former CSA victim/witnesses involved in legal cases, having been arrested was associated with more negative feelings about the effects of the CSA case, greater dissatisfaction with the outcome of the CSA case, and more negative feelings about the legal system's treatment of individuals' accused of crime. These associations highlight how multiple experiences across individuals' lives must be considered when evaluating their current perceptions, both about specific prior experiences and their feelings more generally. Given that many child victims of maltreatment, including CSA, have contact with the legal system as defendants, both in juvenile and criminal court (see Farrington & Loeber, 2000; Quas, Bottoms, & Nunez, 2002; Thornberry et al., 2001; Widom & White, 1997), it is imperative to continue to investigate how different types of experiences (i.e., as victims and perpetrators of crime) shape individuals' emerging beliefs about the legal system and justice.

Summary

Overall, our findings are consistent with the idea that the consequences of childhood stress—in this case legal involvement—change over the course of development and as a function of the child's reactions to and experiences during the stressor. Trial characteristics were also important, although often in complicated ways. Finally, the associations between age and legal involvement on later mental health and attitudes held even when other child and proximal characteristics, which themselves had implications for outcomes, were considered. The next step is to develop more specific models of long-term functioning in CSA survivors who have been involved in criminal prosecutions. It will also be important to determine whether such models generalize to other childhood stressors that affect long-term mental health and feelings about prior negative life experiences.

CAVEATS AND LIMITATIONS

Several caveats and limitations of our study should be noted. The first concerns separation of the effects of legal involvement from those of abuse. As mentioned, our study was not designed to identify the long-term consequences of CSA. Nor could we isolate the effects of legal involvement per se in analyses including the nonabused control group. To address this latter problem, we would need to compare participants in the present study with a group of CSA victims whose abuse was not prosecuted and to a group of individuals who, as children, testified for reasons other than their own victimization (e.g., child witnesses to homicide, domestic violence, or serious accidents). Additional problems, however, would be inherent in such an attempt. For instance, CSA victims without legal involvement likely differ from our participants for reasons besides prosecution: It is quite reasonable to expect systematic differences between cases that are and are not brought to the attention of the criminal courts (e.g., severity, presence of corroboration, willingness of the victim to disclose). Also, children who testified for other reasons may not be easily located, as children are not asked nearly as often to take the stand for other crimes as for CSA (Goodman et al., 1999). Even if found, these children would likely not be comparable with child victims on other relevant variables (i.e., age, SES, initial behavioral adjustment). Finally, to the extent that one of our primary goals was to understand the consequences of legal involvement specifically among CSA victims, a valid approach is to examine outcomes that are associated with different degrees of legal involvement.

Second, some might question whether the child victim/witnesses in our study were true CSA victims (e.g., perhaps the former allegations were false) and whether the nonabused controls were successfully screened for CSA (e.g., perhaps they failed to remember or report former abuse). Although it is impossible to know the full range of the legal involvement sample's experiences, their CSA cases had been screened by law enforcement officials and then by prosecutors in an attempt to rule out false reports. Moreover, although the original cases were brought to the attention of the legal system in the 1980s, a time when several sensational preschool and ritual abuse cases were also being prosecuted—many of which are now largely believed to have been based on false or highly exaggerated reports—our sample included no large preschool CSA cases or ritual abuse allegations. It should be noted that, although a few participants in the current study ($n = 3$) indicated that the target CSA case was based on a false report, our findings hold when those cases are eliminated. Moreover, it is unclear if these claims are false denials of actual abuse or accurate portrayals of previous false allegations.

With regard to the nonabused control group, all possible participants were screened for childhood experiences of CSA. Their caregivers were asked about CSA and about the adolescent or young adult's victimization history, providing a second wave of screening for the controls. Six individuals reported CSA and were subsequently excluded from the sample. As mentioned earlier, it is still possible that a few of the control participants included in the final sample had also experienced CSA. For instance, they may not have remembered their prior experiences of CSA, or they and their caregivers may have elected, during their participation in the current study, not to report the incidents. Such a pattern of results would likely increase the similarity between the legal involvement and control groups (because some of the latter experienced CSA), thereby reducing our ability to identify effects of legal involvement following child sexual victimization. Thus, our findings may be somewhat conservative.

Third, as in the original Goodman et al. (1992) study, we could not randomly assign participants to testifying versus nontestifying groups, or to CSA versus nonabused control groups. As a result, our findings are largely correlational, meaning that causality cannot be inferred. For instance, we cannot conclude that testifying per se caused a particular outcome, although the longitudinal nature of our quasi-experimental design helps reduce some constraints relevant to causation. Also, although we attempted to control for possible confounding factors in our analyses, there is always the possibility that some other unmeasured variable contributed to our results. For instance, individual-difference characteristics related to appraisal processes, intelligence, temperament, or biological reactivity may have implications for some of the outcomes we studied. Furthermore, characteristics of the offenders (e.g., violent habitual criminals) not captured in our study could have affected our findings (e.g., concerning case outcome).

Unfortunately, we could not measure all possible intervening experiences between the legal case and current study that may have affected individuals' current functioning and attitudes about the legal system. However, our findings suggest that legal involvement and the experience of testifying (or not testifying under certain circumstances) may lead children down developmental pathways that themselves affect later functioning (e.g., Sameroff & Chandler, 1975). The study of these pathways and the ways in which experiential factors influence this particularly vulnerable group of children is an important avenue for future research.

Fourth, caution should be taken with regard to the generalizability of our results. For one, we do not know whether our results generalize to jurisdictions other than those in and around Denver, Colorado, or to time periods other than the 1980s. There are reasons to believe that the courts in this area were more sensitive than other courts to children's vulnerabilities. For instance, major centers for treatment and prevention of child abuse and neglect are located in this area. In addition, Colorado statutes allowed some discretion for the use of special practices and special evidentiary rules in CSA cases (Melton, 1992). Yet, children were heard more frequently at preliminary hearings in these jurisdictions than in many others, which may cause distress to the child early in the prosecution. Our findings need to be replicated in other longitudinal studies to confirm their robustness. Further, to the extent that the courts may have (quite arguably) become kinder, more gentle places, results for child victim/witnesses today might differ.

Despite some concerns regarding generalizability, our sample was representative of the 1992 sample. We included more than 80% of the original sample in Phase 1, and minimal differences emerged between individuals who did and did not complete this phase. Across the individual, legal, and proximal characteristics, only gender differed, with females being more likely than males to take part in Phase 1. Thus, findings concerning the Phase 1 measures do not appear dependent on overt biases in participation rates. Participants who completed Phase 2 were also largely representative of the original sample, although they experienced less severe abuse and were less closely related to the perpetrator than those who did not complete Phase 2. It is worth noting that the trauma-specific mental health measures were collected during Phase 2. One could thus speculate that the findings reported here (e.g., increased defensive avoidance among individuals who testified against a parent) would have been stronger had more participants who were closely related to the perpetrator been included. It is also possible that more direct associations, for instance between abuse invasiveness and long-term outcomes, may have emerged.

Finally, our results, like those of virtually all longitudinal studies, are dependent upon the original study sample, measures, and procedures. The same caveats that apply to the original study are still true today (e.g., only some families initially agreed to participate, partial reliance on parent report). For instance, children whose families elected to take part in the 1992 study were less closely related to the perpetrator and were more likely to have received maternal support following abuse discovery. Proportionally more families of male than female victims agreed to participate and, in a few instances, the District Attorney (DA) asked that particular families not be contacted because of an already tenuous relationship with the DA office. Thus, our analyses may provide a particularly rosy picture of the long-term consequences of criminal involvement, in part because the original child participants may have come from better functioning, more supportive families than those who did not participate, especially families involved in intrafamilial abuse cases. We were also not able to assess, from the original study, participants' control over the decision to testify. That is, we do not know if they chose or refused to testify.

Fortunately, we were able to overcome one limitation of the original 1992 study, specifically its exclusive reliance on the CBCL, completed by parents or primary caregivers, as the index of the victim/witnesses' behavioral adjustment. In the current study, we collected measures not only from caregivers, but also from the participants themselves. That the findings varied somewhat depending on the reporter demonstrates the importance of multiple informants when identifying long-term outcomes associated with legal involvement following CSA.

Conclusions and Next Steps

In closing, participation in a CSA criminal case may have both positive and negative consequences for CSA victims, in the short and long term. Our findings reveal that, when evaluating these outcomes, it is imperative to take into account children's age at the time of the legal involvement, whether they testified repeatedly, and a number of other risk factors. Moreover, the associations between legal involvement and outcomes vary with age: Although younger victims may be at increased risk for some adverse outcomes (e.g., mental health problems), older victims may be at increased risk for other undesirable sequelae (e.g., negative attitudes). These outcomes must be interpreted within frameworks that account for individuals' reactions to stress and trauma as well as their perceptions of justice. Findings from the present study can also be used to support changes in legal practice that minimize disadvantages and maximize the advantages of testifying. For instance, greater educational and support efforts should be undertaken to ensure that children are prepared throughout the legal process, whether or not they testify. Without abjuring legal rights necessary to protect defendants, legal professionals and policy makers may want to modify court procedures to make testifying less stressful, both in the short and the long term.

117

REFERENCES

Achenbach, T. M. (1994). Child Behavior Checklist and related instruments. In M. E. Mariush (Ed.), *The use of psychological testing for treatment planning and outcome assessment* (pp. 517–549). Hillsdale, NJ: Erlbaum.

Achenbach, T. M. (1997). *Manual for the young adult self-report and young adult behavior checklist.* Burlington, VT: Department of Psychiatry, University of Vermont.

Achenbach, T. M. (1999). The Child Behavior Checklist and related instruments. In M. Maruish (Ed.), *The use of psychological testing for treatment planning and outcomes assessment* (2nd ed., pp. 429–466). Mahwah, NJ: Lawrence Erlbaum Associates, Inc.

Achenbach, T. M., & Edelbrock, C. (1981). Behavioral problems and competence reported by parents of normal and disturbed children aged 4–16. *Monographs of the Society for Research in Child Development, 46,* 1–198.

Achenbach, T. M., & Rescorla, L. A. (2003). *Manual for ASEBA adult forms & profiles.* Burlington, VT: University of Vermont, Research Center for Children, Youth, & Families.

Alexander, K. W., Quas, J. A., Goodman, G. S., Ghetti, S., Edelstein, R. S., Redlich, A. D., Cordon, M., & Jones, D. P. H. (2005). Traumatic impact predicts long-term memory for documented child sexual abuse. *Psychological Science, 16,* 33–40.

Arata, C. M. (2002). Child sexual abuse and sexual revictimization. *Clinical Psychology: Science and Practice, 9,* 135–164.

Ashworth, C. D., & Feldman-Summers, S. (1978). Perceptions of the effectiveness of the criminal justice system: The female victims' perspectives. *Criminal Justice and Behavior, 5,* 227–240.

Bagley, C. (1996). A typology of child sexual abuse: The interaction of emotional, physical and sexual abuse as predictors of adult psychiatric sequelae in women. *Canadian Journal of Human Sexuality, 5,* 101–112.

Bartholomew, K., & Horowitz, L. M. (1991). Attachment styles among young adults: A test of a four-category model. *Journal of Personality and Social Psychology, 61,* 226–244.

Batterman-Faunce, J. M., & Goodman, G. S. (1993). Effects of context on the accuracy and suggestibility of child witnesses. In G. S. Goodman & B. L. Bottoms (Eds.), *Child victims, child witnesses: Understanding and improving testimony* (pp. 301–330). New York, NY: Guilford Press.

Berliner, L. (2004). Protecting society from dangerous sex offenders: Law, justice and therapy. *Child Maltreatment: Journal of the American Professional Society on the Abuse of Children, 9,* 429–431.

Berliner, L., & Conte, J. R. (1995). The effects of disclosure and intervention on sexually abused children. *Child Abuse and Neglect, 19,* 371–384.

Berliner, L., & Elliot, D. M. (2002). Child sexual abuse. In J. E. B. Myers, L. Berliner, J. Briere, C. T. Hendrix, J. Carole & T. A. Reid (Eds.), *The APSAC handbook on child maltreatment* (2nd ed., pp. 64–101). Thousand Oaks, CA: Sage Publications.

Bernstein, E. M., & Putnam, F. W. (1986). Development, reliability, and validity of a dissociation scale. *Journal of Nervous and Mental Disease*, **174**, 727–735.

Bill, D. F. (1995). *The effect of testifying in court on children who have been sexually abused.* Unpublished doctoral dissertation, The Fielding Institute.

Block, S., Oran, D., Goodman, G. S., & Oran, H. (2005). *Maltreated children's knowledge and attitudes about dependency court.* Paper presented at the American Psychology-Law Society Convention, La Jolla, CA.

Bottoms, B. L. (1993). Individual differences in perceptions of child sexual assault victims. In G. S. Goodman & B. L. Bottoms (Eds.), *Child victims, child witnesses: Understanding and improving testimony* (pp. 229–261). New York, NY: Guilford Press.

Bottoms, B. L., & Goodman, G. S. (1994). Evaluation of children's testimony: Factors influencing the jury. *Journal of Applied Social Psychology*, **24**, 702–732.

Bowlby, J. (1980). *Attachment and loss: Vol. 3. Loss.* New York: Basic Books.

Briere, J., Elliott, D. M., Harris, K., & Cotman, A. (1995). Trauma symptom inventory: Psychometrics and association with childhood and adult victimization in clinical samples. *Journal of Interpersonal Violence*, **10**, 387–401.

Bronfenbrenner, U. (1979). *Ecology of human development: Experiments by nature and design.* Cambridge, MA: Harvard University Press.

Bronfenbrenner, U., & Morris, P. (1998). The ecology of developmental processes. In W. Damon & R. M. Lerner (Eds.), *Handbook of child psychology* (Vol. I). New York: Wiley.

Browne, A., & Finkelhor, D. (1986). Impact of child sexual abuse: A review of the research. *Psychological Bulletin*, **99**, 66–77.

Bruck, M., & Ceci, S. (2004). Forensic developmental psychology. *Current Directions in Psychological Science*, **13**, 229–232.

Burchinal, M. R., Roberts, J. E., Hooper, S., & Zeisel, S. A. (2000). Cumulative risk and early cognitive development: A comparison of statistical risk models. *Developmental Psychology*, **36**, 793–807.

Case, R. (1991). *The mind's staircase: Exploring the conceptual underpinnings of children's thought and knowledge.* Hillsdale, NJ: Lawrence Erlbaum Associates, Inc.

Cashmore, J., & Bussey, K. (1989). Children's conception of the witness role. In J. Spencer, R. Nicholson, R. Flin & R. Bull (Eds.), *Children's evidence in legal proceedings* (pp. 177–188). Cambridge: University of Cambridge.

Cederborg, A. C., & Lamb, M. (2004). Delay of disclosure, minimization, and denial of abuse in a multi-victim case. In M. Lamb (Chair), *Delayed and non-disclosure of child sexual abuse in forensic interviews*. Symposium conducted at the American Psychology-Law Society Conference. Scottsdale, AZ.

Celano, M. P. (1992). A developmental model of victims' internal attributions of responsibility for sexual abuse. *Journal of Interpersonal Violence*, **7**, 57–69.

Cicchetti, D., & Lynch, M. (1993). Toward an ecological/transactional model of community violence and child maltreatment: Consequences for children's development. *Psychiatry: Interpersonal and Biological Processes*, **56**, 96–118.

Cicchetti, D., & Rogosch, F. A. (1999). Conceptual and methodological issues in developmental psychopathology research. In P. C. Kendall & J. N. Butcher (Eds.), *Handbook of research methods in clinical psychology* (2nd ed., pp. 433–465). New York, NY, U.S.: John Wiley & Sons, Inc.

Cicchetti, D., & Toth, S. L. (1995). A developmental psychopathology perspective on child abuse and neglect. *Journal of the American Academy of Child and Adolescent Psychiatry*, **34**, 541–565.

Compas, B. E. (1987). Coping with stress during childhood and adolescence. *Psychological Bulletin*, **101**, 393–403.

Conte, J. R., & Berliner, L. (1984). *The Sexual Assault Profile*. Unpublished document.

Conte, J. R., & Berliner, L. (1988). The impact of sexual abuse on children: Empirical findings. In L. E. Walker (Ed.), *Handbook on sexual abuse of children: Assessment and treatment* (pp. 72–93). New York: Springer.

Croog, S. H., Levine, S., Testa, M. A., Brown, B., Bulpitt, C. J., Jenkins, C. D., Klerman, G. L., & Williams, G. H. (1986). The effects of antihypertensive therapy on quality of life. *New England Journal of Medicine*, **314**, 1657–1664.

Coy v. Iowa (1988). 487 U.S. 1012.

Dahlquist, L. M., Power, T. G., Cox, C. N., & Fernbach, D. J. (1994). Parenting and child distress during cancer procedures: A multidimensional assessment. *Children's Health Care*, **23**, 149–166.

Davis, E., Quas, J. A., Horowitz, B., Wallin, A. & Lyon, T. D. (2005). *Maltreated children's knowledge of dependency court*. Paper presented at the American Psychology-Law Society Convention, La Jolla, CA.

Deater-Deckard, K., Dodge, K. A., Bates, J. E., & Pettit, G. S. (1998). Multiple risk factors in the development of externalizing behavior problems: Group and individual differences. *Development and Psychopathology*, **10**, 469–493.

DeFrancis, V. (1969). *Protecting the child victim of sex crimes committed by adults*. Denver, CO: American Humane Association.

Derogatis, L. R. (1993). Brief Symptom Inventory: Administration, scoring, and procedures manual (4th ed.). Minneapolis, MN: National Computer Systems, Inc.

Derogatis, L. R., & Lazarus, L. (1994). SCL-90–R, Brief Symptoms Inventory, and matching clinical rating scales. In M. E. Mariush (Ed.), *The use of psychological testing for treatment planning and outcome assessment* (pp. 217–248). Hillsdale, NJ: Erlbaum.

Derogatis, L. R., & Melisaratos, N. (1983). The Brief Symptom Inventory: An introductory report. *Psychological Medicine*, **3**, 595–605.

Dodge, K. A., Bates, J. E., & Pettit, G. S. (1990). Mechanisms in the cycle of violence. *Science*, **250**, 1678–1683.

Dodge, K. A., & Price, J. M. (1994). On the relation between social information processing and socially competent behavior in early school-aged children. *Child Development*, **65**, 1385–1897.

Downey, G., & Feldman, S. I. (1996). Implications of rejection sensitivity for intimate relationships. *Journal of Personality and Social Psychology*, **70**, 1327–1343.

Dubester, K. A., & Braun, G. (1995). Psychometric properties of the Dissociative Experiences Scale. *Journal of Nervous and Mental Disease*, **183**, 231–235.

Edelstein, R. S., Ghetti, S., Quas, J. A., Goodman, G. S., Alexander, K. W., Redlich, A. D., & Cordon, I. M. (in press). Individual differences in emotional memory: Adult attachment and long-term memory for child sexual abuse. *Personality and Social Psychology Bulletin*.

Edwards, V. J., Holden, G. W., Felitti, V. J., & Anda, R. F. (2003). Relationship between multiple forms of childhood maltreatment and adult mental health in community respondents: Results from the adverse childhood experiences study. *American Journal of Psychiatry*, **160**, 1453–1460.

Egeland, B. R., Carlson, E., & Sroufe, L. A. (1993). Resilience as process. *Development and Psychopathology*, **5**, 517–528.

Egeland, B., Yates, T., Appleyard, K., & van Dulmen, M. (2002). The long-term consequences of maltreatment in the early years: A developmental pathway model to antisocial behavior. *Children's Services: Social Policy, Research, and Practice*, **5**, 249–260.

Ehrensaft, M. K., Cohen, P., Brown, J., Smailes, E., Chen, H., & Johnson, J. G. (2003). Intergenerational transmission of partner violence: A 20-year prospective study. *Journal of Consulting and Clinical Psychology*, **71**, 741–753.

Elder, G. H. Jr., & Caspi, A. (1988). Human development and social change: An emerging perspective on the life course. In A. Caspi & M. M. Downey (Eds.), *Persons in context: Developmental processes* (pp. 77–113). New York: Cambridge University Press.

Elder, G. H. Jr., & Conger, R. D. (2000). *Children of the land: Adversity and success in rural America*. Chicago: University of Chicago Press.

Elliott, D. S., & Ageton, S. S. (1980). Reconciling race and class differences in self-reported and official estimates of delinquency. *American Sociological Review*, **45**, 95–110.

Enright, R. D., Enright, W. F., & Lapsley, D. K. (1981). Distributive justice development and social class. *Developmental Psychology*, **17**, 826–832.

Entwisle, D. R., & Astone, N. M. (1994). Some practical guidelines for measuring youth's race/ethnicity and socioeconomic status. *Child Development*, **65**, 1521–1540.

Essex, M. J., Klein, M. H., Miech, R., & Smider, N. A. (2001). Timing of initial exposure to maternal major depression and children's mental health symptoms in kindergarten. *British Journal of Psychiatry*, **179**, 151–156.

Farrington, D. P., & Loeber, R. (2000). Epidemiology of juvenile violence. *Child and Adolescent Psychiatric Clinics of North America*, **9**, 733–748.

Feiring, C., Taska, L., & Lewis, M. (1999). Age and gender differences in children's and adolescents' adaptation to sexual abuse. *Child Abuse and Neglect*, **23**, 115–128.

Ferguson, B. (1979). Preparing young children for hospitalization: A comparison of two methods. *Pediatrics*, **64**, 656–664.

Finkelhor, D. (1979). What's wrong with sex between adults and children? Ethics and the problem of sexual abuse. *American Journal of Orthopsychiatry*, **49**, 692–697.

Finkelhor, D. (1984). Sexual abuse in the national incidence of child abuse and neglect: An appraisal. *Child Abuse and Neglect*, **8**, 23–32.

Fischer, K. W. (1980). A theory of cognitive development: The control and construction of hierarchies of skills. *Psychological Review*, **87**, 477–531.

Flin, R. H. (1992). Child witnesses in Scottish trials. In F. Loesel & D. Bender (Eds.), *Psychology and law: Facing the nineties* (pp. 365–373). Amsterdam: Swets & Zeitlinger.

Foa, E. B., Cashman, L., Jaycox, L., & Perry, K. (1997). The validation of a self-report measure of posttraumatic stress disorder: The posttraumatic diagnostic scale. *Psychological Assessment*, **9**, 445–451.

Folger, R. (1977). Distributive and procedural justice: Combined impact of voice and improvement on experienced inequity. *Journal of Personality and Social Psychology*, **35**, 108–119.

Fontaine, R., Salvano-Pardieu, V., Crouzet, S., & Pulford, B. D. (2002). Physically abused and nonmaltreated boys' moral judgements of violence. *Child Study Journal*, **32**, 215–230.

Freshwater, K., & Aldridge, J. (1994). The knowledge and fears about court of child witnesses, schoolchildren and adults. *Child Abuse Review*, **3**, 183–195.

Friedrich, W. N., & Reams, R. A. (1987). Course of psychological symptoms in sexually abused young children. *Psychotherapy: Theory, Research, Practice, Training*, **24**, 160–170.

Friedrich, W. N., Urquiza, A. J., & Beilke, R. L. (1986). Behavior problems in sexually abused young children. *Journal of Pediatric Psychology*, **11**, 47–57.

Furstenberg, Cook, Eccles, Elder, & Sameroff (1999). *Managing to make it: Urban families and adolescent success*. Chicago, IL: University of Chicago.

Ghetti, S., Edelstein, R. S., Goodman, G. S., Quas, J. A., Alexander, K., Redlich, A. D., Cordon, I. M., & Jones, D. P. (in press). What can subjective forgetting tell us about memory for childhood trauma? *Memory and Cognition*.

Gilliom, M., Shaw, D. S., Beck, J. E., Schonberg, M. A., & Lukon, J. L. (2002). Anger regulation in disadvantaged preschool boys: Strategies, antecedents, and the development of self-control. *Developmental Psychology*, **38**, 222–235.

Glaser, D., & Spencer, J. R. (1990). Sentencing, children's evidence and children's trauma. *Criminal Law Review*, 371–382.

Gold, L. J., Darley, J. M., Hilton, J. L., & Zanna, M. P. (1984). Children's perceptions of procedural justice. *Child Development*, **55**, 1752–1759.

Goldstein, N. E. S., Condie, L. O., Kalbeitzer, R., Osman, D., & Geier, J. L. (2003). Juvenile offenders' Miranda rights comprehension and self-reported likelihood of offering false confessions. *Assessment*, **10**, 359–369.

Goodman, G. S., Bottoms, B. L., Rudy, L., Davis, S., & Schwartz-Kenney, B. M. (2001). Effects of past abuse experiences on children's eyewitness memory. *Law and Human Behavior*, **25**, 235–256.

Goodman, G. S., Ghetti, S., Quas, J. A., Edelstein, R., Alexander, K., Redlich, A. D., Cordon, I., & Jones, D. P. (2003). A prospective study of memory for child sexual abuse: New findings relevant to the repressed memory controversy. *Psychological Science*, **14**, 113–118.

Goodman, G. S., Hirschman, J. E., Hepps, D., & Rudy, L. (1991). Children's memory for stressful events. *Merrill-Palmer Quarterly*, **37**, 109–157.

Goodman, G. S., Jones, D. P., & Pyle, E. A. (2003). The emotional effects of criminal court testimony on child sexual assault victims: A preliminary report. *Issues in Criminological and Legal Psychology*, **13**, 46–54.

Goodman, G. S., Quas, J. A., Batterman-Faunce, J. M., & Kuhn, G. (1997). Children's reactions to and memory for a stressful event: Influences of age, anatomical dolls, knowledge, and parental attachment. *Applied Developmental Science*, **1**, 54–75.

Goodman, G. S., Quas, J. A., Batterman-Faunce, J. M., Riddlesberger, M. M., & Kuhn, J. (1994). Predictors of accurate and inaccurate memories of traumatic events experienced in childhood. *Consciousness and Cognition*, **3**, 269–294.

Goodman, G. S., Quas, J. A., Bulkley, J., & Shapiro, C. (1999). Innovations for child witnesses: A national survey. *Psychology, Public Policy, and Law*, **5**, 255–281.

Goodman, G. S., Taub, E. P., Jones, D. P. H., England, P., Port, L. K., Rudy, L., & Prado, L. (1992). Testifying in criminal court. *Monographs of the Society for Research in Child Development*, **57** (5, Serial No. 229).

Grant, K. E., Compas, B. E., Stuhlmacher, A. F., Thurm, A. E., McMahon, S. D., & Halpert, J. A. (2003). Stressors and child and adolescent psychopathology: Moving from markers to mechanisms of risk. *Psychological Bulletin*, **129**, 447–466.

Gray, E. (1993). *Unequal justice: The prosecution of child sexual abuse*. New York, NY: Free Press.

Haugaard, J. J., & Reppucci, N. D. (1988). *The sexual abuse of children: A comprehensive guide to current knowledge and intervention strategies*. San Francisco, CA, U.S.: Jossey-Bass.

Henry, J. (1997). System intervention trauma to child sexual abuse victims following disclosure. *Journal of Interpersonal Violence*, **12**, 499–512.

Hexel, M., Wiesnagrotzki, S., & Sonneck, G. (2004). Psychiatric disorders and traumatic life events. *German Journal of Psychiatry*, **7**, 28–34.

Hicks, A. J., & Lawrence, J. A. (1993). Children's criteria for procedural justice: Developing a young people's procedural justice scale. *Social Justice Research*, **6**, 163–182.

Hoffman-Plotkin, D., & Twentyman, C. T. (1984). A multimodal assessment of behavioral and cognitive deficits in abused and neglected preschoolers. *Child Development*, **55**, 794–802.

Huizinga, D., & Elliot, D. (1983). A preliminary examination of the reliability and validity of the national youth survey-self-reported delinquency indices. *National Youth Survey, Project Report* 27. Boulder CO: Behavioral Research Institute.

Indermaur, D. (1994). Offenders' perceptions of sentencing. *Australian Psychologist*, **29**, 140–144.

Jackson, Y., & Warren, J. S. (2000). Appraisal, social support, and life events: Predicting outcome behavior in school-age children. *Child Development*, **71**, 1441–1457.

Katz, S., & Mazur, M. A. (1979). *Understanding the rape victim*. New York: Wiley.

Kellogg, N. D. (2002). Child sexual abuse: A marker or magnifying glass for family dysfunction? *Social Science Journal*, **39**, 569–582.

Kendall-Tackett, K. A., Williams, L. M., & Finkelhor, D. (1993). Impact of sexual abuse on children: A review and synthesis of recent empirical studies. *Psychological Bulletin*, **113**, 164–180.

Kohlberg, L. (1968). The child as a moral philosopher. *Psychology Today*, **2**, 25–30.

Koop, C. E. (1989). Responding to the patient who has AIDS. *Academic Medicine*, **64** (3), 113–115.

Kraemer, H. C., Measelle, J. R., Ablow, J. C., Essex, M. J., Boyce, W. T., & Kupfer, D. J. (2003). A new approach to integrating data from multiple informants in psychiatric assessment and research: Mixing and matching contexts and perspectives. *American Journal of Psychiatry*, **160**, 1566–1577.

LaBouvie-Vief, G. (1998). Cognitive-emotional integration in adulthood. In K. W. Schaie & M. P. Lawton (Eds.), *Annual review of gerontology and geriatrics: Vol. 17. Focus on emotion and adult development* (pp. 206–237). New York, NY: Springer Publishing Co.

Lazarus, R. S. (1991). Progress on a cognitive-motivational-relational theory of emotion. *American Psychologist*, **46**, 819–834.

Leadbeater, B. J., Kuperminc, G. P., Blatt, S. J., & Hertzog, C. (1999). A multivariate model of gender differences in adolescents' internalizing and externalizing problems. *Developmental Psychology*, **35**, 1268–1282.

Lind, E. A., & Tyler, T. R. (1988). *The social psychology of procedural justice*. NY: Plenum Press.

Little, R. J. A., & Rubin, D. R. (1989). The analysis of social science data with missing values. *Sociological Methods and Research*, **18**, 292–326.

Livingston, R. (1987). Sexually and physically abused children. *Journal of the American Academy of Child and Adolescent Psychiatry*, **26**, 413–415.

Marx, B. P., & Sloan, D. M. (2003). The effects of trauma history, gender, and race on alcohol use and posttraumatic stress symptoms in a college student sample. *Addictive Behaviors*, **28**, 1631–1647.

Maryland v. Craig (1990). 497 U.S. 836, 110 S. Ct. 3157.

Masten, A. S., & Coatsworth, J. D. (1998). The development of competence in favorable and unfavorable environments: Lessons from research on successful children. *American Psychologist*, **53**, 205–220.

Masten, A. S., & Wright, M. O. (1998). Cumulative risk and protection models of child maltreatment. *Journal of Aggression, Maltreatment and Trauma*, **2**, 7–30.

Maughan, A., & Cicchetti, D. (2002). Impact of child maltreatment and interadult violence on children's emotion regulation abilities and socioemotional adjustment. *Child Development*, **73**, 1525–1542.

Maughan, B., & Rutter, M. (1998). Continuities and discontinuities in antisocial behavior from childhood to adult life. *Advances in Clinical Child Psychology*, **20**, 1–47.

McGillicuddy-DiLisi, A. V., Watkins, C., & Vinchur, A. J. (1994). The effect of relationship on children's distributive justice reasoning. *Child Development*, **65**, 1694–1700.

Melton, G. B. (1992). Children as partners for justice: Next steps for developmentalists. *Monographs of the Society for Research in Child Development*, **57** (5, Serial No. 229), 153–159.

Melton, G. B., & Berliner, L. (1992, April). *Preparing sexually abused children for testimony: Children's perceptions of the legal process (Final Report)*. Washington, DC: National Center on Child Abuse and Neglect.

Melton, G. B., Goodman, G. S., Kalichman, S. C., Levine, M., Saywitz, K. J., & Koocher, G. P. (1995). Empirical research on child maltreatment and the law. *Journal of Clinical Child Psychology*, **24**, 47–77.

Merritt, K. A., Ornstein, P. A., & Spicker, B. (1994). Children's memory for a salient medical procedure: Implications for testimony. *Pediatrics*, **94**, 17–23.

Messer, J., Maughan, B., Quinton, D., & Taylor, A. (2004). Precursors and correlates of criminal behaviour in women. *Criminal Behaviour and Mental Health*, **14**, 82–107.

Moffitt, T. E. (1993). Adolescence-limited and life-course-persistent antisocial behavior: A developmental taxonomy. *Psychological Review*, **100**, 674–701.

Nathanson, R., & Saywitz, K. J. (2003). The effects of the courtroom context on children's memory and anxiety. *Journal of Psychiatry and Law*, **31**, 67–98.

NICHD Early Child Care Research Network (2004). Trajectories of physical aggression from toddlerhood to middle childhood. *Monographs of the Society for Research in Child Development*, **69**, vii-129.

Oates, K., & Tong, L. (1987). Sexual abuse of children: An area with room for professional reform. *Medical Journal of Australia*, **147**, 544–548.

Oran, H. S. (1989). *Abused and neglected children in juvenile court: A study of their attitudes, knowledge, state anxiety, and concerns.* Unpublished doctoral dissertation, University of California, Los Angeles.

Overton, R. C. (1998). A comparison of fixed-effects and mixed (random-effects) models for meta-analysis tests of moderator variable effects. *Psychological Methods*, **3**, 354–379.

Overton, W. F., & Horowitz, H. A. (1991). Developmental psychopathology: Integrations and differentiations. In D. Cicchetti & S. L. Toth (Eds.), *Rochester symposium on developmental psychopathology: Vol. 3. Models and integrations* (pp. 1–42). Rochester, NY: University of Rochester.

Parke, R. D. (1995). Fathers and families. In M. H. Bornstein (Ed.), *Handbook of parenting: Vol. 3. Status and social conditions of parenting* (pp. 27–63). Hillsdale, NJ: Lawrence Erlbaum.

Peterson, C. (1995). The role of perceived intention to deceive in children's and adults' concepts of lying. *British Journal of Developmental Psychology*, **13**, 237–260.

Peterson, C., & Bell, M. (1996). Children's memory for traumatic injury. *Child Development*, **67**, 3045–3070.

Piaget, J. (1932). *The moral judgment of the child*. London: Kegan Paul.

Quas, J. A., Bottoms, B. L., & Nunez, N. (2002). Child maltreatment and delinquency: Framing issues of causation and consequence. *Children's Services: Social Policy, Research, &Practice*, **5**, 245–248.

Quas, J. A., Goodman, G. S., & Jones, D. (2003). Predictors of attributions of self-blame in child sexual abuse victims. *Journal of Child Psychology and Psychiatry and Allied Disciplines*, **44**, 723–746.

Redlich, A. D., Alexander, K., Goodman, G. S., Quas, J. A., Ghetti, S., & Edelstein, R. (2000, March). *Relations between child sexual abuse and juvenile delinquency: Findings from a prospective study of children and adolescents involved in the legal system.* Poster presented at the American Psychology-Law Society Conference, New Orleans, LA.

Redlich, A. D., Silverman, M., & Steiner, H. (2003). Pre-adjudicative and adjudicative competence in juveniles and young adults. *Behavioral Sciences and the Law*, **21**, 393–410.

Reimer, M. S., Overton, W. F., Steidl, J. H., Rosenstein, D. S., & Horowitz, H. (1996). Familial responsiveness and behavioral control: Influences on adolescent psychopathology, attachment, and cognition. *Journal of Research on Adolescence*, **6**, 87–112.

Rohner, R. P. (2004). The parental "acceptance-rejection syndrome": Universal correlates of perceived rejection. *American Psychologist*, **59**, 830–840.

Rudd, M. D., Joiner, T. E. J., & Rumzek, H. (2004). Childhood diagnoses and later risk for multiple suicide attempts. *Suicide and Life-Threatening Behavior*, **34**, 113–125.

Runyan, D. K., Everson, M. D., Edelsohn, G. A., Hunter, W. M., & Coulter, M. L. (1988). Impact of legal intervention on sexually abused children. *Journal of Pediatrics*, **113**, 647–653.

Russell, D. E. H. (1986). *The secret trauma: Incest in the lives of girls and women* (2nd ed.). NY: Basic Books.

Rutter, M. (1971). Normal psychosexual development. *Journal of Child Psychology and Psychiatry and Allied Disciplines*, **11**, 259–283.

Rutter, M. (1979). Maternal deprivation, 1972–1978: New findings, new concepts, new approaches. *Child Development*, **50**, 283–305.

Rutter, M. (1983). Prevention of children's psychosocial disorders: Myth and substance. *Annual Progress in Child Psychiatry and Child Development*, 271–295.

Rutter, M., & Quinton, D. (1977). Psychiatric disorders: Ecological factors and concepts of causation. In H. McGurk (Ed.), *Ecological factors in human development* (pp. 173–187). Amsterdam, Holland: North-Holland.

Sahjpaul, S., & Renner, K. E. (1988). The new sexual assault law: The victim's experience in court. *American Journal of Community Psychology*, **16**, 503–513.

Sameroff, A. J., & Chandler, M. J. (1975). Reproductive risk and the continuum of caretaker casualty. In F. D. Horowitz (Ed.), *Review of child development research* (Vol. 4). Chicago: University of Chicago Press.

Sameroff, A. J., Seifer, R., Baldwin, A., & Baldwin, C. (1993). Stability of intelligence from preschool to adolescence: The influence of social and family risk factors. *Child Development*, **64**, 80–97.

Sameroff, A. J., Seifer, R., Zax, M., & Barocas, R. (1987). Early indicators of developmental risk: Rochester longitudinal study. *Schizophrenia Bulletin*, **13**, 383–394.

Sánchez, M. M., Ladd, C. O., & Plotsky, P. M. (2001). Early adverse experience as a developmental risk factor for later psychopathology: Evidence from rodent and primate models. *Development and Psychopathology*, **13**, 419–449.

Sas, L. D. (1991). *Reducing the system-induced trauma for child sexual abuse victims through court preparation, assessment, and follow-up*. London: London Family Court.

Sas, L. D. (1993). *Three years after the verdict*. Ontario, Canada: London Family Court Clinic.

Sattar, G., & Bull, R. (1996). Pre-court preparation for child witnesses. *Issues in Criminological and Legal Psychology*, **26**, 67–75.

Saywitz, K. J. (1989). "Court is a place you play basketball": Children's knowledge of the legal system. In S. J. Ceci, D. Ross & M. Toglia (Eds.), *Perspectives on children's testimony*. New York: Springer.

Saywitz, K., Jaenicke, C., & Camparo, L. (1990). Children's knowledge of legal terminology. *Law and Human Behavior*, **14**, 523–535.

Seltzer, M. L., Vinokur, A., & Van Rooijen, L. J. (1975). A self-administered Short Michigan Alcohol Screening Test (SMAST). *Studies on Alcohol*, **36**, 117–126.

Sigelman, C. K., & Waitzman, K. A. (1991). The development of distributive justice orientations: Contextual influences on children's resource allocations. *Child Development*, **62**, 1367–1378.

Smetana, J. G., Toth, S. L., Cicchetti, D., Bruce, J., Kane, P., & Daddis, C. (1999). Maltreated and nonmaltreated preschoolers' conceptions of hypothetical and actual moral transgressions. *Developmental Psychology*, **35**, 269–281.

Smiljanich, K., & Briere, J. (1993). *Sexual abuse history and trauma symptoms in a university sample*. Paper presented at the Annual Meeting of the American Psychological Association, Toronto, Canada.

Spaccarelli, S. (1994). Stress, appraisal, and coping in child sexual abuse: A theoretical and empirical review. *Psychological Bulletin*, **116**, 340–362.

Tebbutt, J., Swanston, H., Oates, R. K., & O'Toole, B. I. (1997). Five years after child sexual abuse: Persisting dysfunction and problems of prediction. *Journal of the American Academy of Child and Adolescent Psychiatry*, **36**, 330–339.

Tedesco, J., & Schnell, S. (1987). Children's reactions to sex abuse investigation and litigation. *Child Abuse and Neglect*, **11**, 267–272.

Thibaut, J., & Walker, L. (1975). *Procedural justice: A psychological analysis*. Hillsdale, NJ: Erlbaum.

Tompkins, B. M., & Olejnik, A. B. (1978). Children's reward allocations: The impact of situational and cognitive factors. *Child Development*, **49**, 526–529.

Tong, L., Oates, K., & McDowell, M. (1987). Personality development following sexual abuse. *Child Abuse and Neglect*, **11**, 371–383.

Trickett, P. K., & Putnam, F. W. (1993). Impact of child sexual abuse on females: Toward a developmental, psychobiological integration. *Psychological Science*, **4**, 81–87.

Tufts New England Medical Center, Division of Psychiatry (1984). *Sexually exploited children: Service and research project*. Final report for the Office of Juvenile Justice and Delinquency Prevention. Washington, DC: U.S. Department of Justice.

Tyler, T. R. (1984). The role of perceived injustice in defendents' evaluations of their courtroom experience. *Law and Society Review*, **18**, 51–74.

Tyler, T. R. (1988). Criteria used by citizens to assess the fairness of legal procedures. *Law and Society Review*, **22**, 104–135.

Tyler, T. R. (1994). Psychological models of the justice motive: Antecedents of distributive and procedural justice. *Journal of Personality and Social Psychology*, **67**, 850–863.

Tyler, T. R., & Degoey, P. (1995). Community, family, and the social good: The psychological dynamics of procedural justice and social identification. In G. B. Melton (Ed.), *The individual, the family, and social good: Personal fulfillment in times of change* (pp. 53–91). Lincoln, NE: Nebraska University Press.

Tyler, T. R., & Folger, R. (1980). Distributional and procedural aspects of satisfaction with citizen-police encounters. *Basic and Applied Social Psychology*, **1**, 281–292.

Tyler, T. R., & Lind, E. A. (1992). A relational model of authority in groups. *Advances in Experimental Social Psychology*, **25**, 115–191.

Tyler, T. R., & Lind, E. A. (2001). Procedural justice. In J. Sanders & V. L. Hamilton (Eds.), *Handbook of justice research in law* (pp. 65–92). Dordrecht, Netherlands: Kluwer Academic Publishers.

Umbreit, M. S. (1989). Crime victims seeking fairness, not revenge: Toward restorative justice. *Federal Probation*, **53**, 52–57.

U.S. Department of Health and Human Services (2002). *Child maltreatment 2000*. Washington, DC: Government Printing Office.

Warren-Leubecker, A., Tate, C., Hinton, I., & Ozbek, N. (1989). What do children know about the legal system and when do they know it? In S. Ceci, M. Toglia & D. Ross (Eds.), *Perspectives on children's testimony* (pp. 158–183). New York: Springer.

Weissman, M. M. (1978). Social adjustment by self-report in a community sample and in psychiatric outpatients. *Journal of Nervous and Mental Disease*, **166** (5), 317–326.

Weissman, M. M., & Bothwell, S. (1976). Assessment of social adjustment by patient self report. *Archives of General Psychiatry*, **33**, 1111–1115.

Werner, E. E. (1987). Vulnerability and resiliency in children at risk for delinquency: A longitudinal study from birth to young adulthood. In J. D. Burchard & S. N. Burchard (Eds.), *Prevention of delinquent behavior* (pp. 16–43). Thousand Oaks, CA: Sage.

Werner, E. E., & Smith, R. S. (1992). *Overcoming the odds: High risk children from birth to adulthood*. Ithaca, NY, U.S.: Cornell University.

Whitcomb, D., Runyan, D. K., DeVos, E., Hunter, W. M., Cross, T. P., Everson, M. D., Peeler, N. A., Porter, C. Q., Toth, P. A., & Cropper, C. (1991). *Child victims as witnesses: Research and development program*. Final report to the Office of Juvenile Justice and Delinquency Prevention. Washington, DC.

Widom, C. S. (1991). The role of placement experiences in mediating the criminal consequences of early childhood victimization. *American Journal of Orthopsychiatry*, **61**, 195–209.

Widom, C. S., & White, H. R. (1997). Problem behaviours in abused and neglected children grown up: Prevalence and co-occurrence of substance abuse, crime and violence. *Criminal Behaviour and Mental Health*, **7**, 287–310.

Williams, S., Anderson, J., McGee, R., & Silva, P. A. (1990). Risk factors for behavioral and emotional disorder in preadolescent children. *Journal of the American Academy of Child and Adolescent Psychiatry*, **29**, 413–419.

Wolfe, D. A., Wolfe, V. V., & Best, C. L. (1988). Child victims of sexual abuse. In V. B. Van Hasselt & R. L. Morrison (Eds.), *Handbook of family violence* (pp. 157–185). New York, NY: Plenum.

ACKNOWLEDGMENTS

This article is based upon work supported by the National Science Foundation under Grant No. 0004369. Any opinions, findings, conclusions, or recommendations expressed in this article are those of the authors and do not necessarily reflect the views of the National Science Foundation. We thank Stephanie Block, Deena Day, Patricia England, Jenny Garfein, Jennifer Noll, Linda Port, Lydia Prado, Juliana Raskauskas, Leslie Rudy, Jennifer Schaaf, Phillip R. Shaver, Steven Shirk, Daniel Stroski, Elizabeth Pyle Taub, Penelope Trickett, Allison Wallin, and the many undergraduate students at the University of California, Davis, and graduate students at the University of Denver who provided their assistance. Thanks are also given to Sally Murphy and her interview team at the National Opinion Research Center for help with data collection. We are grateful to the staff at the Adams, Arapahoe, and Denver County District Attorney Offices. Special thanks go to District Attorneys James Peters, Robert Grant, and William Ritter, and Deputy District Attorneys John Jordan, Jill Straus, and Norman Brisson. Gina Gallo and Lois Buckman also offered valuable assistance. Finally, our sincerest gratitude is expressed to the individuals, especially the former child victims, who took part in our research. For correspondence contact Dr. Jodi Quas at Department of Psychology and Social Behavior, 3340 Social Ecology II, University of California, Irvine, 92697-7085 (949-824-7693) or Dr. Gail Goodman at Department of Psychology, University of California, One Shields Avenue, Davis, CA 95616 (530-752-6981).

E-mail: jquas@uci.edu; ggoodman@ucdavis.edu.

IMPLICATIONS OF LONGITUDINAL RESEARCH WITH CHILD WITNESSES FOR DEVELOPMENTAL THEORY, PUBLIC POLICY, AND INTERVENTION STRATEGIES

Jeffrey J. Haugaard

The sexual abuse of a child usually involves a process. The process often begins before a sexually abusive act occurs, as a potential perpetrator identifies a child who might be abused and begins to create a condition conducive to future abuse, such as giving the child special attention or gifts, using sexual themes in conversation, or engaging in physical contact such as hugging. If the perpetrator begins to engage in sexually abusive behavior, the behavior may gradually increase in intensity, sometimes to the point of frequent intercourse (e.g., Goodman, Emery, & Haugaard, 1998). If an abused child reveals the abuse and the abuse is reported to legal authorities, a cascade of events begins. Child protective agency staff members or the police interview the child, possibly several times, and members of a district attorney's staff may also interview the child. The child will experience reactions from parents and siblings, and possibly peers, teachers, and others if the abuse becomes public knowledge. There may be disruptions in the child's home life, the child may be placed in foster care, and the child may become involved in family or criminal court proceedings. Each component of this cascade may have short term or long term, positive or negative influences on the child's development.

Our knowledge of the forms that this process can take has grown over the past few decades, although there is still much that we do not know. The study presented in this monograph is one of the few that has examined the influence of the cascade of events that occurs after sexual abuse is reported to legal authorities. The long-standing research program, of which this study is part, is unique in that it has examined the influence of these events over many years of a child's development. Thus, it provides one of the few glimpses that we have into the ways that a child's legal involvement can influence his or her development.

This study presents information that can inform research, developmental theory, public policy, and interventions for sexually abused children and their families. In this commentary, I focus on some of the many findings of this study that I found to provide novel information. I also describe some findings for which I have struggled, unsuccessfully, to understand their meaning, and conclude with a list of characteristics of children, and their proximal and distal environments, that may be the focus of future research that will enhance the information from the research described in this monograph.

THE RESEARCH PROCESS

This study demonstrates some obstacles to investigating the consequences of child sexual abuse and shows that useful information can be gathered despite these obstacles. A significant obstacle in a study such as this is that the control of critical variables in the research design, so that the influence of other variables can be assessed, is often impossible. The researchers cannot influence, much less control, what happens to any of the children as they interact with the legal system, and must simply record and try to calculate the importance of the many different experiences that each child has. In addition, the fragile nature of some research participants and the sensitivity of the topic of the research can require modification of the procedures for some participants, as occurred in this study, which can complicate the interpretation of the data.

The authors show that, with sufficient effort, useful information can be gleaned from a study in which researchers have no control over the experiences of the participants. There are limitations to the confidence with which conclusions can be drawn from a study such as this, and the lack of experimental control means that alternate conclusions often cannot be dismissed. However, by providing statistical control of many variables, the researchers have supplied information that confirms the conclusions from other studies (e.g., maternal support improves child outcomes), thus strengthening belief in them, and have supplied information on which new conclusions can be based (e.g., not testifying can lead to negative outcomes for some children). The authors demonstrate that, instead of avoiding studying situations in which each participant has a unique set of characteristics and experiences, valuable information can be gathered about these situations.

A second research issue raised by this study is the difficulty of interpreting results when a person's self-report of his or her behavior differs from someone else's report about the behavior (in this case, mothers are the ones providing reports on their child's behavior). A clear example of this difficulty can be seen in Table 6, where mothers' reports of their child's[4] internalizing symptoms, but not the child's, were correlated with an attitude about the unfairness of the legal system, and where the child's reports of externalizing symptoms, but not the mothers', were correlated with this attitude. This disparity of reports may be due partly to the mothers and their children completing different measures, although each measure claims to assess internalizing and externalizing symptoms.

Disparities between self-reports and parent reports occur regularly in social-science research. For example, mothers often rate the frequency of their school-age children's oppositional behaviors as higher than do their children (Loeber, Green, Lahey, & Stouthamer-Loeber, 1991), and many adolescents report more frequent conduct-disordered behaviors than their mothers report (Boyle, Offord, Racine, & Sanford, 1993; Loeber, Burke, Lahey, Winters, & Zera, 2000). Disparities also occur when assessing internalizing symptoms, as parents may be unaware of their children's internalizing symptoms if their children do not share this information with them (e.g., "Nothing is wrong, mom!!") (Cole, Tram, Martin, Hoffman, Ruiz, & Jacquez, 2002). One intriguing study that focused on depressive symptoms in adolescents had clinicians interview mothers and adolescents individually, using the K-SADS. They divided the mother/adolescent pairs into three groups (a) where the results from the adolescent interviews only were positive for depression, (b) where the results from the mother interviews only were positive for depression, and (c) where the results from both the adolescent and the mother were positive for depression. The adolescents who were the most depressed were identified by both themselves and their mothers, those with moderate depression were identified only by their mothers, and those with lower levels of depression were identified only by themselves (Braaten, Biederman, DiMauro, Mick, Monuteaux, & Muehl, 2001).

At issue is how to interpret these disparate reports. One of my few disagreements with the authors of this monograph is that they appear to focus on reports that correlate with outcome measures whatever the source of the report. For example, they note that internalizing symptoms are associated with increased beliefs about the unfairness of the legal system based on the mothers' reports, even though the self-reports of internalizing symptoms from the participants were not correlated with the attitude. I raise this issue not to argue with the authors' interpretation of their findings, but to note that there is little empirically based guidance for researchers who must interpret disparate reports from different informants. This basic research issue is one that is in need of empirical investigation, and it may be that strategies that are useful for handling disparate reports for one type of symptom or group of symptoms may not be useful for handling disparate reports about other types or groups of symptoms.

131

DEVELOPMENTAL THEORY

Several findings from this study support current developmental theories, such as the differences between boys and girls in their externalizing and internalizing problems and the role that maternal support has on children's responses to stressful situations. Two findings were particularly interesting.

One result related to the changing beliefs over time that some children had about their court involvement. The findings showed that some children who experienced a positive reaction to not testifying at the time of the trial of their alleged perpetrator experienced a negative reaction several years later to not having testified. The findings highlight how children's cognitions about an event can change over time, probably due in part to their developing cognitive abilities and in part to their experiences. They also show that measuring beliefs or feelings about an event at one point in time does not tell the full story, and that ongoing measurement is required to determine whether those beliefs or feelings change. This finding is similar to the one reported by Brodzinsky and his colleagues in their study of children who had been adopted as infants or toddlers (Brodzinsky, 1987). They found that the children's beliefs about what it meant to be adopted became more negative during their school-age years than during their preschool years. Their analysis of the children's explanations of what it meant to be adopted led them to hypothesize that the change was due to the school-age children's ability to hold two beliefs in mind (I was chosen specially by my adoptive parents; before that I was abandoned [rejected] by my birth mother) whereas younger children typically held only one belief (I was chosen specially by my adoptive parents).

The second finding that was particularly intriguing is shown in Figure 5. The authors assessed the consequences of testifying multiple times, which has been shown in this and other studies to be more problematic than testifying once or not at all, on the participants' externalizing symptoms at the time of the follow-up study. They found a significant interaction between testifying and improvement in functioning during their earlier study period (reported in Goodman, Taub, Jones, England, Port, Rudy, & Prado, 1992) on the children's externalizing symptoms at the follow-up assessment. Among those whose functioning had improved during the initial study period, those who testified multiple times had higher levels of mother-reported externalizing symptoms than those who did not testify. However, among those whose functioning had not improved, there was no association between testifying and externalizing symptoms. Thus, it appears that the children who had begun to recover from the negative consequences of their abuse and their involvement with the legal system were particularly vulnerable to the long-term consequences of testifying multiple times.

As described in the monograph, many studies have shown that it is usually the accumulation of risk factors, rather than experiencing any particular risk factor, that puts children at greater risk for negative outcomes (Rutter, 1979; Sameroff, Seifer, Zax, & Barocas, 1987). This study suggests that counting the number of events that are risk factors may not be sufficient, and that it may also be important to assess the child's response to each event. The study suggests that children who "buck up" and improve after experiencing the negative consequences of a stressful event may respond more negatively to another stressful event occurring soon afterward than do children whose functioning does not improve after the first stressful event. Children who can work themselves through two or three stressful events may be particularly vulnerable to a fourth one occurring soon afterwards. This reminds me of the Greek myth in which a person has been punished by the gods by having to roll a boulder up a hill repeatedly, because the boulder rolls back down each time right before the summit is reached. How often can children be expected to roll the boulder of their mental health up a hill if, after nearing the summit another stressful event sends the boulder back down? Perhaps some variability in outcomes seen among children who have experienced the same number of risk factors is influenced by the improvement they attain after experiencing the earlier risk factors: those who improve may experience more negative long-term outcomes from their accumulated risks than those who have not improved after the first one or two. This suggests that measuring a child's response to stressors may be as important as measuring the frequency and intensity of the stressors.

PUBLIC POLICY

The most obvious implication for public policy from this study is that, as in most public-policy issues, there are no simple answers—in this case to the question of whether children should be discouraged, allowed, or encouraged to testify against a person on trial for sexually abusing them. Too often, it seems, public policy is based on simple answers to complex questions. This study shows that answers to questions such as whether it is harmful for children to testify is a more complex "maybe." Some children appear to benefit from testifying while others appear to be harmed by it. Consequently, each case is unique and blanket assertions about the benefit or harm of testifying are inappropriate. The study provides information that furthers our understanding of when it is more likely to be harmful or helpful for children to testify, but more work is needed before we can begin to identify with more certainty the characteristics of children, their abuse, and their environments that are associated with better or worse outcomes of either testifying or not testifying.

The finding that older children had a more difficult experience while testifying than younger children suggests that the procedures that some courts have used to reduce the stress of testifying for young victims of sexual abuse, such as allowing them to have a parent nearby or encouraging judicial restraint on attorneys as they question the child, should be applied to older children as well. This study suggests that, if the motivation to use procedures that reduce stress on young children when they testify comes from society's concern about the welfare of children, then these procedures should be extended to older children who must testify (perhaps in modified form). If our concern is only about the welfare of young children, then current procedures may be adequate; if our concern is for all potentially vulnerable children, then procedures to reduce the stress of testifying should be expanded.

The long-term consequences of high levels of distress while waiting to testify that were reported in this study suggest that procedures to provide a reduced-stress environment for children as they await testifying are needed. As these procedures would be unrelated to the child's time in court, they could be implemented without concern for the effect that they might have on a defendant's rights. As I read the monograph, I could picture these children sitting in the hallway of a courthouse, surrounded by activity and sure that everyone who looked at them knew why they were there and what had been done to them (or worse, what they had done). My heart went out to them. It must be like sitting in the school office waiting to see the principal because of some rule infraction, with teachers and other students wandering through and knowing that you had been "bad," only more intense. Separate rooms where children and their families could wait, with activities for the child or even a radio playing, would be easy to construct and may be of long-term benefit to children who must testify in court.

As seen in other studies (e.g., Goodman et al., 1992; Whitcomb, Runyan, DeVos, Hunter, Cross, Everson, Peeler, Porter, Toth, & Cropper, 1991), children who are interviewed more times and who must testify more times are at greater risk for negative outcomes. The negative consequences of multiple interviews have been addressed in the past by videotaping the first interview or two with a child, and then having those videotapes available to others who may need to learn the information coming from the interviews. The goal of this procedure was to reduce the number of times that a child had to provide details about the abuse. I have learned from colleagues who are attorneys, however, that videotaping early interviews is done less frequently now, because conflicting information recorded during the interviews, or conflicts between the videotaped interviews and a child's court testimony, can be used by the defendant to call into question the accuracy of the child's testimony. Consequently, more children may now be subject to repeated interviews.

INTERVENTIONS

The most obvious implication of this study for interventions with sexually abused children and their families, either by mental-health professionals or those working in the courts, is that helping a child and his or her parents understand the potential benefits and liabilities of either testifying or not testifying is important. Some associations between testifying and child outcomes reported in this study cannot be known when discussing the implications of testifying, such as whether a defendant is found guilty or the type of sentence that the defendant receives. However, the characteristics of the children, their abuse experiences, and their family environment that this study found were related to better or worse outcomes, depending on whether a child testified, should be useful in any discussion of a child's potential testimony. In addition, this study shows that those discussing these issues with a child and his or her parents must focus on both short-term and long-term consequences and help the child and parents balance any potential short-term consequences with any potential long-term consequences of either testifying or not.

The results from this study showing that negative attitudes toward the legal system are held by many sexually abused children—particularly females, those severely abused, and those involved in cases where the perpetrator received only a minimal sentence—are distressing. Children who have been sexually abused are at higher risk for being abused again as children and for experiencing sexual abuse or sexual assault as adolescents and adults (Arata, 2002; Haugaard & Reppucci, 1988). Those who have developed negative attitudes toward the legal process from their involvement as a witness in a sexual abuse trial may be less likely to report any future sexual victimization to legal authorities. This suggests that a discussion of attitudes and how they might affect a person's behavior following a future experience of sexual victimization should be an important component of an intervention with a sexually abused child involved in the legal system.

The changes in the children's thinking about their abuse experiences and about their court involvement, noted above, suggest that interventions with abused children who become involved in the legal system need to be long term. Even if a child does not receive therapeutic interventions for an extended period after involvement in a legal case, it may be important for parents or others to monitor a child's beliefs or feelings about the earlier abuse experiences periodically, and seek professional guidance if it appears that a child's thinking or feelings about their experiences are becoming problematic.

Finally, the result from this and other studies about the importance of maternal support on children's adjustment after revealing sexual abuse is a reminder that interventions with family members are often an essential part of the services received by a child who has been sexually abused. Although most studies focus on maternal support, the support of fathers, siblings, and members of the extended family may also be important, and so they may need to be involved in services as well.

A CONFUSING FINDING

A result that I found confusing is seen in Figure 4, showing an interaction between testifying and sentence severity on externalizing symptoms. Among children who had not testified, there were no significant differences in their externalizing symptoms based on whether the defendant had received a lenient or severe sentence. However, children who had testified multiple times exhibited more externalizing symptoms if the defendant had received a severe sentence than if the defendant had received a lenient sentence. One might think that children who had to testify multiple times (which was shown to be more stressful), and who then saw the defendant receive a lenient sentence, might experience more negative consequences than those who saw the defendant receive a more severe sentence, as they could justify the stress they endured by the sentence received by the defendant. However, the results show just the opposite. The authors hypothesize that the positive consequences of seeing the defendant receive a severe sentence were overshadowed by the negative consequences associated with testifying multiple times, but this does not explain why these children had a higher level of symptoms than those who testified multiple times and then saw the defendant receive a lenient sentence (two potential negative consequences). What it is about the interaction between testifying multiple times and seeing the defendant receive a severe sentence that is associated with a more negative outcome eludes me.

FUTURE RESEARCH

The authors of this monograph have collected an extensive amount of data on the characteristics and experiences of the research participants. All researchers know that there is a limit to the amount of accurate data that can be gathered from people who volunteer as research participants and that it can be difficult determining what potentially important information should be gathered and what should not. That said, I found myself wondering about the potential influence of several individual, family, and neighborhood characteristics on the short- and long-term outcomes of sexually abused children involved in the legal system. Obtaining information about these and other characteristics in future studies of children involved as trial witnesses may expand our knowledge about them and their ongoing development.

Information about personality and/or temperament characteristics of the child may provide additional insights into which children respond more positively or negatively to involvement in the legal system. For example, children who are more introverted, anxious about novel situations, or pessimistic may react to involvement with the legal system in a more negative way than other children. To the extent that personality/temperament characteristics are associated with reactions to involvement in the legal system, knowledge of these characteristics could provide important information to those working with individual children before or after any legal involvement.

Given the important role that maternal support has on the outcomes of sexually abused children, some additional information about the associations between characteristics and experiences of mothers and their ability to provide support to their children could be helpful. In a broad sense, knowing about the mother's personality and any history of psychological disorders may be helpful. More narrowly, knowing if the mother was a victim of sexual abuse or assault as a girl or adult, whether she had been the victim of domestic violence, or whether she had any involvement with the police may provide some insights into her level of support for her sexually abused child once they all become involved with the legal system. Further, information on the strength of the social support that the mother receives, and its association with the support she provides her abused child, may be useful. To the extent that associations between these or other characteristics or experiences of the mother are associated with her level of support for her abused child, it may be possible to identify mothers who are at risk for providing little support to their abused child and to work with them to give them what they need to be more supportive.

Knowing about the amount and value of the support available to a sexually abused child from sources other than his or her mother would provide a fuller picture of the value of social support to a child. Support from fathers, siblings, extended family members, and other adults (e.g., teachers) may also be helpful to a sexually abused child, particularly a child who receives little support from his or her mother.

Knowing about the amount of family disruption resulting from the abuse or from the child's and family's legal involvement may provide important additional information about influences on the short- and long-term consequences to the child. For example, loss of income if an abusive father is jailed or required to leave the family, the family's need to move to another home or apartment, possibly requiring the child to change schools, and consequences to the siblings of the abused child, which may influence their relationship with the child, may all provide useful information about the consequences that the child experiences as the result of the abuse and consequently his or her response to it and to legal involvement.

Finally, knowing about neighborhood attitudes toward the legal system may lead to a better understanding of the attitudes that children have about their legal involvement. Children from neighborhoods where the police are seen as protectors and as fair and beneficial may enter any legal involvement with different beliefs than those from neighborhoods where there is little support for the police and other legal authorities. These initial beliefs may have an important influence on the long-term attitudes that the children have about the legal system.

NOTE

4. For clarity, I use the term *child* to refer to the person who was abused, despite the fact that some of them were adolescents or young adults at the time of this study.

References

Arata, C. M. (2002). Child sexual abuse and sexual revictimization. *Clinical Psychology: Science and Practice*, **9**, 135–164.

Boyle, M. H., Offord, D. R., Racine, Y., & Sanford, M, ET AL. (1993). Evaluation of the Diagnostic Interview for Children and Adolescents for use in general population samples. *Journal of Abnormal Child Psychology*, **21**, 663–681.

Braaten, E. B., Biederman, J., DiMauro, A., Mick, E., Monuteaux, M. C., Muehl, K., & Farune, S. (2001). Methodological complexities in the diagnosis of major depression in youth: An analysis of mother and youth self-reports. *Journal of Child and Adolescent Psychopharmacology*, **11**, 395–407.

Brodzinsky, D. M. (1987). Adjustment to adoption: A psychosocial perspective. *Clinical Psychology Review*, **7**, 25–47.

Cole, D. A., Tram, J. M., Martin, J. M., Hoffman, K. B., Ruiz, M. D., Jacquez, F. M., Farrah, M., & Maschman, T. (2002). Individual differences in the emergence of depressive symptoms in children and adolescents: A longitudinal investigation of parent and child reports. *Journal of Abnormal Psychology*, **111** (1), 156–165.

Goodman, G., Emery, R., & Haugaard, J. J. (1998). Developmental psychology and the law: Divorce, child maltreatment, foster care, and adoption. In I. Sigel, & A. Renninger (Eds.) *Handbook of child psychology. Volume 4: Child psychology in practice* (5th ed., pp. 775–876). New York: Wiley.

Goodman, G., Taub, E. P., Jones, D. P. H., England, P., Port, L. K., Rudy, L., & Prado, L. (1992). Testifying in criminal court. *Monographs of the Society for Research in Child Development*, **57** (5, Serial No. 229), 1–142.

Haugaard, J. J., & Reppucci, N. D. (1988). *The sexual abuse of children: A comprehensive guide to current knowledge and intervention strategies*. San Francisco: Jossey–Bass.

Loeber, R., Burke, J. D., Lahey, B. B., Winters, A., & Zera, M. (2000). Oppositional defiant and conduct disorder: A review of the past 10 years, Part I. *Journal of the American Academy of Child and Adolescent Psychiatry*, **39**, 1468–1484.

Loeber, R., Green, S. M., Lahey, B. B., & Stouthamer-Loeber, M. (1991). Differences and similarities between children, mothers, and teachers as informants on disruptive child behavior. *Journal of Abnormal Child Psychology*, **19**, 75–95.

Rutter, M. (1979). Maternal deprivation, 1972–1978: New findings, new concepts, new approaches. *Child Development*, **50**, 283–305.

Sameroff, A. J., Seifer, R., Zax, M., & Barocas, R. (1987). Early adverse experience as a developmental risk factor for later psychopathology: Evidence from rodent and primate models. *Development and Psychopathology*, **13**, 419–449.

Whitcomb, D., Runyan, D. K., DeVos, E., Hunter, W. M., Cross, T. P., Everson, M. D., Peeler, N. A., Porter, C. Q., Toth, P. A., & Cropper, C. (1991) *Child victims as witnesses: Research and development program*. Final report to the Office of Juvenile Justice and Delinquency Prevention, Washington, DC.

CONTRIBUTORS

Kristen W. Alexander (Ph.D., 2002, University of California, Davis) received her doctoral degree in Human Development. She is currently Assistant Professor at California State University, Sacramento. Her research interests focus broadly on cognitive development as it relates to children's ability to attend to and later remember stressful personal experiences. Her studies have focused on the development of different forms of memory, children's memory for stressful experiences, and sources of individual differences in children's episodic memory. Her most recent research concerns the relations among attachment, executive function, electrophysiological responses, and emotional memories in children and adults.

Ingrid Cordon (Ph.D., 2004, University of California, Davis) is currently a postdoctoral fellow at Harvard University. Her research interests concern the ontogeny and development of memory in early childhood. Specifically, she is interested in the relations between language, emotion, and memory, as well as in the effects of trauma on memory development. Her current program of research examines the functional and neural development of the explicit memory system in both typically developing children and children with suspected damage to the hippocampus (a structure critical for explicit memory). To investigate the development of explicit memory and to identify the neural networks that support memory processes, Dr. Cordon employs both behavioral (e.g., explicit memory tasks, neuropsychological tests) and electrophysiological methods. Her research has been funded by the National Science Foundation and the American Psychological Association.

Robin Edelstein (Ph.D., 2005, University of California, Davis) is a postdoctoral fellow at the University of California, Irvine. Her research interests fall in two main areas: the influence of emotion on memory, including individual differences in memory for emotional material, and

140

attachment-related differences in the regulation of emotion, cognition, and behavior. To address these issues, Dr. Edelstein has conducted experimental, longitudinal, and correlational studies of emotional memory in both children and adults. She has also examined individual differences (e.g., in adult attachment and mental health) in emotional memory, as well as attachment-related differences in behavior in emotional situations. Her research has been supported by awards from the American Psychological Association and the American Psychological Foundation.

Simona Ghetti (Ph.D., 2002, University of California, Davis) currently has a joint appointment as Assistant Professor at the University of California, Davis, and as a Research Scientist at the National Research Council in Bologna, Italy. Her primary research interest concerns the processes underlying the formation and rejection of false memories. In one line of research, Dr. Ghetti investigates the extent to which individuals make metamemory-based inferences when rejecting false memories (e.g., "If something like this had happened, then I would remember it"). In another line of research, she investigates developmental trends in the mechanisms involved in false-memory formation and rejection. Other studies focus on the subjective experience of remembering, the relation between trauma and memory, and children's and adolescents' involvement as victims and defendants in the legal system. Dr. Ghetti's research is currently funded by the National Science Foundation.

Gail S. Goodman (Ph.D., 1977, University of California, Los Angeles) is Professor of Psychology and Director of the Center for Public Policy Research at the University of California, Davis, and Professor of Forensic Psychology at the University of Oslo, Norway. Dr. Goodman's research falls into two major areas: memory development and children's abilities and experiences as victim/witnesses. In the memory development area, her work explores theoretical issues concerning the relations between memory and emotion, trauma, and attachment. In the victim/witness area, her research focuses on children's ability to provide testimony about events they have experienced or witnessed, especially events related to child abuse, and on the psychological effects of testifying in court. Dr. Goodman has served as president of two divisions (Division 37, Child, Youth, and Family Services; and Division 41, Psychology and Law) and one section (Child Maltreatment) of the American Psychological Association. She has received many grants and awards, including two Distinguished Contributions awards in 2005 from the American Psychological Association (the Distinguished Contributions to Research in Public Policy Award, and the Distinguished Professional Contributions to Applied Research Award). After obtaining her Ph.D. in Developmental Psychology, Dr. Goodman conducted postdoctoral research at the University of Denver and the Université René Descartes in Paris, France.

David P. H. Jones (D.C.H., 1978, M.R.C. Psych 1980, University of Birmingham) is a Consultant Child and Family Psychiatrist and Senior Lecturer, University of Oxford, at the Park Hospital for Children, Oxford. He leads a multi-disciplinary child psychiatric clinical team providing services for abused children and their families. He has researched and published widely in the fields of child abuse and neglect, children's reactions to trauma, and consent to treatment among children.

Jodi A. Quas (Ph.D., 1998, University of California, Davis) is Assistant Professor in the Department of Psychology and Social Behavior at the University of California, Irvine. After obtaining her Ph.D., she spent 2 years as a postdoctoral fellow in the Institute of Human Development at the University of California, Berkeley. Her research has two main foci: memory development and children's involvement in the legal system. She has examined such questions as how children's memory abilities are influenced by their behavioral and physiological responses to stress, and how social contextual influences affect children's eyewitness memory and suggestibility. She has also examined child victims' coping with and understanding of legal involvement and the use of innovative practices to accommodate child victim/witnesses. Her work has been supported by grants from the National Institute of Child Health and Human Development and the U.S. Department of Health and Human Services. For her contributions to the field of developmental psychology and the law, Dr. Quas has received early career awards from Divisions 9 (Society for the Psychological Study of Social Issues) and 41 (American Psychology—Law Society) of the American Psychological Association.

Allison D. Redlich (Ph.D., 1999, University of California, Davis) received her doctoral degree in Developmental Psychology. She then spent 3 years as a postdoctoral fellow in the Department of Psychiatry at Stanford University. Dr. Redlich is currently a research associate at Policy Research Associates, Inc. Her research is broadly focused on the legal system's response to and accommodation of vulnerable populations of both victims and defendants. Of particular interest for her is juvenile interrogation by police, and whether certain interrogation tactics lead to false confessions. Dr. Redlich has also conducted research on the effects of hearsay in legal cases involving children, and attitudes toward child sexual abuse prevention measures. She is currently PI or co-PI of two multi-site investigations of the use of mental health courts, funded by the National Science Foundation and the MacArthur Foundation.

Jeffrey Haugaard (Ph.D., 1990, Clinical Psychology, University of Virginia). He is currently Stephen Weiss Presidential Fellow and associate professor in the Department of Human Development at Cornell University. Dr. Haugaard was the founding president of the Section on Child Maltreatment of the American Psycyhological Association and is currently the representative to the American Psychological Association's Council of Representatives from the Division of Child, Youth, and Family Services. His current research focuses on stalking and other forms of intrusive contact that can occur when adolescent and young–adult romantic relationships end, although he continues to write about areas of earlier research including child maltreatment and the adoption of school-age children. He has recently published a set of clinical guides: *Recognizing and Treating Behavioral and Emotional Disorders in Severely Maltreated Children and Adolescents*.

STATEMENT OF EDITORIAL POLICY

The *Monographs* series is devoted to publishing developmental research that generates authoritative new findings and uses these to foster fresh, better integrated, or more coherent perspectives on major developmental issues, problems, and controversies. The significance of the work in extending developmental theory and contributing definitive empirical information in support of a major conceptual advance is the most critical editorial consideration. Along with advancing knowledge on specialized topics, the series aims to enhance cross-fertilization among developmental disciplines and developmental sub fields. Therefore, clarity of the links between the specific issues under study and questions relating to general developmental processes is important. These links, as well as the manuscript as a whole, must be as clear to the general reader as to the specialist. The selection of manuscripts for editorial consideration, and the shaping of manuscripts through reviews-and-revisions, are processes dedicated to actualizing these ideals as closely as possible.

Typically *Monographs* entail programmatic large-scale investigations; sets of programmatic interlocking studies; or—in some cases—smaller studies with highly definitive and theoretically significant empirical findings. Multi-authored sets of studies that center on the same underlying question can also be appropriate; a critical requirement here is that all studies address common issues, and that the contribution arising from the set as a whole be unique, substantial, and well integrated. The needs of integration preclude having individual chapters identified by individual authors. In general, irrespective of how it may be framed, any work that is judged to significantly extend developmental thinking will be taken under editorial consideration.

To be considered, submissions should meet the editorial goals of *Monographs* and should be no briefer than a minimum of 80 pages (including references and tables). There is an upper limit of 175–200 pages. In exceptional circumstances this upper limit may be modified. (Please submit four copies.) Because a *Monograph* is inevitably lengthy and usually substantively complex, it is particularly important that the text be well organized and written in clear, precise, and literate English. Note, however, that authors from non-English-speaking countries should not be put off by this stricture. In accordance with the general aims of SRCD, this series is actively interested in promoting international exchange of developmental research. Neither membership in the Society nor affiliation with the academic discipline of psychology are relevant in considering a *Monographs* submission.

The corresponding author for any manuscript must, in the submission letter, warrant that all coauthors are in agreement with the content of the manuscript. The corresponding author also is responsible for informing all coauthors, in a timely manner, of manuscript submission, editorial decisions, reviews received, and any revisions recommended. Before publication, the corresponding author also must warrant in the submission letter that the study has been conducted according to the ethical guidelines of the Society for Research in Child Development.

Potential authors who may be unsure whether the manuscript they are planning would make an appropriate submission are invited to draft an outline of what they propose, and send it to the Editor for assessment. This mechanism, as well as a more detailed description of all editorial policies, evaluation process, and format requirements can be found at the Editorial Office web site (http://astro.temple.edu/-overton/monosrcd.html) or by contacting the Editor, Wills F. Overton, Temple University-Psychology, 1701 North 13th St. – Rm 567, Philadelphia, PA 19122-6085 (e-mail: monosrcd@temple.edu) (telephone: 1-215-204-7360).

Monographs of the Society for Research in Child Development (ISSN 0037-976X), one of two publications of Society of Research in Child Development, is published four times a year by Blackwell Publishing with offices at 350 Main St, Malden, MA 02148 USA and PO Box 1354, Garsington Rd, Oxford, OX4 2DQ, UK and PO Box 378 Carlton South, 3053 Victoria, Australia. A subscription to *Monographs of the SRCD* comes with a subscription to *Child Development* (published bimonthly).

INFORMATION FOR SUBSCRIBERS For new orders, renewals, sample copy requests, claims, changes of address and all other subscription correspondences please contact the Journals Department at your nearest Blackwell office (address details listed above). UK office phone: +44 (0) 1865-778315, Fax: +44 (0) 1865-471775, Email: customerservices@oxon.blackwellpublishing.com; US office phone: 800-835-6770 or 781-388-8200, Fax: 781-388-8232, Email: subscrip@bos.blackwellpublishing.com; Asia office phone: +61 3 9347 0300, Fax: +61 3 9347 5001, Email: subscriptions@blackwellpublishingasia.com

INSTITUTIONAL PREMIUM RATES* FOR MONOGRAPHS OF THE SRCD/CHILD DEVELOPMENT 2005 The Americas $449, Rest of World £319. Customers in Canada should add 7% GST to The Americas price or provide evidence of entitlement to exemption. Customers in the UK and EU should add VAT at 5% or provide a VAT registration number or evidence of entitlement to exemption.

*Includes print plus premium online access to the current and all available backfiles. Print and online-only rates are also available.

BACK ISSUES Back issues are available from the publisher at the current single issue rate.

MICROFORM The journal is available on microfilm. For microfilm service, address inquiries to ProQuest Information and Learning, 300 North Zeeb Road, Ann Arbor, MI 48106-1346, USA. Bell and Howell Serials Customer Service Department: (800) 521-0600 × 2873.

ADVERTISING For advertising information, please visit the journal's website at www.blackwellpublishing.com/mono or contact the Academic and Science, Advertising Sales Coordinator, at journaladsUSA@bos.blackwellpublishing.com. 350 Main St. Malden, MA 02148. Phone: 781.388.8532, Fax: 781.338.8532.

MAILING Periodical postage paid at Boston, MA and additional offices. Mailing to rest of world by DHL Smart & Global Mail. Canadian mail is sent by Canadian publications mail agreement number 40573520. Postmaster: Send all address changes to Monographs of the Society for Research in Child Development, Blackwell Publishing Inc., Journals Subscription Department, 350 Main St., Malden, MA 02148-5018.

Sign up to receive Blackwell *Synergy* free e-mail alerts with complete *Monographs of the SRCD* tables of contents and quick links to article abstracts from the most current issue. Simply go to www.blackwellsynergy.com, select the journal from the list of journals, and click on "Sign-up" for FREE email table of contents alerts.

CURRENT